GIRL WITH A FORK IN A WORLD OF SOUP

GIRL
WITH
A FORK
IN A
WORLD
OF SOUP

Rosita Sweetman

ISBN: 978-1-7395705-4-5

MENMA
BOOKS

www.menmabooks.eu

For Chupi and Luke
my dearest darlings, who taught me true love.

'Don't bend; don't water it down; don't try to make it logical, follow your most intense obsessions mercilessly.'

Franz Kafka

PART ONE

1

The first thing I remember is being in Mum's womb. It's crowded because I'm in here with Twin Sister. She's worked herself up into a froth over Mum's visit to the hospital. Mum has been sent for an X-ray because she is 'so big.' Yes, an X-ray. The nurse comes back holding up the large, crackling photographic negative, saying, 'Mrs. Sweetman you'll be delighted to know you're having twins.' Mum, who was never afraid of saying what she felt, says she is not delighted at all. She already has four children at home. That night in the womb Twin Sister is hysterical: Mum hates us, Mum will never ever love us. Mum is a monster, etcetera, etcetera. I spend a long time calming her down. Mum is basically a good person! A good Mum! She's understandably freaked at having not one, but two, more babies. I mean, come on, the poor woman is only human. As soon as we're born everything will be fine. Next thing I remember, we are being born. Twin Sister is in a panic, pounding me with her feet, forcing me out, bum first, so that I come down the birth canal backwards, which is agony for Mum, and terrifying for me: Help Mum! I'm suffocating! I'm yanked forth, towelled down and shoved into a corner while everyone gathers around for delivery of baby number two.

Fifteen minutes later out she comes. 'Would you look at the little rat!' says one of the nurses. Mum, notwithstanding she's just gone through a breach and then a second labour inside of twenty minutes, raises herself up on her elbows and says: 'No one calls a child of mine a rat.' From that moment on, Twin Number Two becomes Twin Number One. She is breast-fed while I get the bottle. She is held close to Mum's warm, warm while I lie numb in the all alone.

Mum!

Years later, Mum said obviously she couldn't feed us both. Obviously? Well, she didn't want to look like some sort of dog, two babies hanging out of her. Even Dad, the kindest man in the world, a barrister, got in on the Second-Born Twin is First act, loudly assuring one and all that the second born twin is legally the eldest. First in terms of inheritance. First in legal terms, primogeniture and so on.

Dad!

It was before Google. Way before the time you could run upstairs, then shout down at them, 'Hey! Google says the first-born twin is legally, and every other way, first. My tiny heart pounded with indignation; it wasn't fair!

Decades later, I meet up with Twin Sister. I tell her about all the re-birthing stuff I've been doing. What I've discovered about being first born, about her being freaked about Mum, and all that. Coincidentally, she says carefully, she has also done some re-birthing therapy sessions. No way! How did she like it? What has she found out? What she remembers most clearly, she says, is directly after being born having this feeling, very strongly, that she'd been given more power than she ought to have, but that she'd decided there and then, no way was she admitting to that, or giving any of it back. I am so excited I almost jump into her face. Really? But she closes down. Not another word can I get out of her. As for our doing a few sessions together, she won't hear of it. Are you mad? No thank you.

2

At first Mum and Dad were happy.

They had their beautiful Georgian house, 'Phoenix Hill,' its toes in the Liffey, Anna Livia Plurabelle, its back to the Phoenix

Park. A wedding present from Granny and Grandfather Sweetman. Their back garden, 1,750 acres of the biggest urban green space in Europe, had herds of deer, stags with their nodding candelabra of horns, does with their young lolling almost hidden in long grass, ears flicking away flies. All theirs to enjoy. In one corner, the Zoological Gardens, pungent with the reek of generations of lion and monkey piss, gibbons hoo-hoo-hooing from their islands, seals barking from their artificial ponds. Then the polo grounds and the cricket grounds, relics of Victoriana with pretty wooden pavilions, the pok-pok of balls meeting wooden bats and sticks.

Mum and Dad snug with their first born and his kitted-out nursery. Dad walking to the Law Library in the morning, Mum setting off on her bicycle at night, light quenched to comply with the war time blackout, to collect butter, sugar and tea coupons our grandmother, Gaga, had saved for her. World War II just over, the war between Mum and Dad not yet begun. Happy days shattered when Dad had a recurrence of TB. Phoenix Hill sold. Mum, heavily and hugely pregnant with us twins, forced to move back in, along with her four other children, to her mother's house in Fitzwilliam Square. Pregnant, furious, penniless, homeless, husbandless. If marriage is a game of snakes and ladders this was Mum and Dad's first snake. Down, down, down they went. Mum raging with Dad for being 'weak,' for getting ill, for forcing the sale of their beautiful Phoenix Hill, for impregnating her again, this time with twins. Dad on a bed on a balcony in Switzerland trying to suck fresh air into his ravaged lungs, scared, ill, alone, miserable.

3

Finally Dad came home from the sanatorium in Switzerland, Twin Sister and I were born, and Mum's much adored aunt, Winifred

Stack, widow of Republican hero Austin Stack, gave her and Dad a present of another house: 'Seabank.' The story of our now six-children-strong family, plus Mum and Dad, began again. Facing out to the wide shallow dish that is Dublin bay, a Napoleonic cut stone Martello tower at one end, a railway crossing, or Merrion Gates, at the other, 'Seabank' was our private Garden of Eden. Here we became a more or less normal 'big' family. Contraception was still strictly forbidden by the Catholic Church. Only Protestants or other non-Catholics had access to packets sent over by friends in the UK, enabling them to limit their brood to 'a gentleman's family' of one or two. Catholics in the meantime were advised—that is, roared at by celibate priests—to use the 'withdrawal' method or the 'rhythm' method. One cruel, the other mostly useless.

I loved being part of a big family. Sandwiched safely in the middle with four bigger ones above me, referred to as 'the others,' Twin Sister and eventually three more, known as 'the littles' below. The clamour and certainty of being in a tribe. The milkman arriving at dawn, the strange hush of his electric van, the chink, chink, chink of the glass bottles in their steel crates, the foil tops pecked open by robins, sipping off the cream on freezing mornings. The boy from the butcher's arriving on his big black messenger boy bike, bloody parcels of meat tied with string. Laundry delivered and collected in creaking baskets, red vans emblazoned SWASTIKA LAUNDRY, Mum saying, 'They really ought to think about changing that.' The pig man collecting 'swills,' a sack around his shoulders, his cart reeking of decaying food. The country girls who came for three months, nine months, depending how long they could stick it. Their rooms smelled of face powder and homesickness. Once, thrillingly, a nanny came from America. 'Auntie B Gavin.' Impeccably dressed in wool suits, a white overcoat—*white!*—she called her bag her 'purse,' the pavements 'sidewalks,' the lifts 'elevators,' the taps 'faucets.'

Sunday lunches with the whole family around the dining table, a roast waiting to be carved by Dad, roast potatoes, two boats of gravy. Winter evenings sitting on the hearth rug in front of a banked turf fire, Dad on one side, Mum on the other, Mum reading, Dad listening, the two of them exchanging glances, trying not to laugh, during the 'smarmy bits': Little Women, Little Lord Fauntleroy and his velvet suit, Little Dorrit. Games in the garden during the summer that went on for days. Us younger ones in our knickers, dragging my eldest sister, 'the Queen,' in her chariot—the wheelbarrow furnished with cushion and rug—while my brother, the overseer, yelled at us, threatened severe whippings. No! Yes! Evenings when us younger ones had to eat in the nursery because a dinner party had been arranged. Preparations all day: the dining room hoovered, the hunting table polished, the two big candelabras carried into the kitchen, the silver laid out on newspaper to be cleaned. Circular crackle glaze bowls crammed with richly scented roses freshly cut from the garden. Out in the orchard with Dad to pick peas and broad beans. Dad digging potatoes, the sharp damp smell of earth as his spade slit open the ground underneath the plants, Dad shaking out the golden 'pommes de terre' for us to pick up and drop into the waiting bucket. Back in the kitchen levering the broad beans out of their long silvery purses, the peas stripped from their pods releasing their fresh green smell, falling like the sound of rain into a white enamel basin. The doorbell ringing. The grown-ups, all dressed up, greeting each other in the hall, chatter in the drawing room as they tuck into the sherry, more chatter as they come down the stairs as the roast is ferried from the kitchen. The big ones allowed to stay up, to pour wine, hand around food. 'Seabank' with its quirky castellated roof. Its wide granite steps, warm to sit on in the summer to watch day trippers dawdling by the sea wall eating ice cream wafers from the Martello tower shop, sadly now shuttered up, the men with rolled-up trousers, heavily veined white legs, handkerchiefs tied in four corners to cover their heads, the women in summer frocks.

'Seabank' with its drawing room at the back, huge windows looking down onto the garden, high granite walls, a greengage tree with white garden table and chairs underneath. A rose garden. A long, fragrant smelling greenhouse where Dad grew tomatoes and marrows. The apple shed, apples carefully stacked on trays for winter, potatoes shrouded under sacks in the darkness below. A rat the size of a small dog, backlit by summer lightning running along the roof, Dad saying, 'They're only dangerous if you corner them.' I think, what if you corner them by accident? What then? At the bottom of the garden a rickety wooden door into the orchard and vegetable garden, where Dad grew sweetcorn, potatoes, french beans, broad beans, runner beans, lettuce. Gooseberry and raspberry bushes, cooking apple trees and eating apple trees, plum trees, peach trees espaliered against warm granite walls. From there a grassy lane that ran back up towards the house. A pussy willow orchard on the left, at the lane top the big tarry black garage where we kept fat-tummied Connemara ponies that we cantered out across the beach, ponies farting from too much grass. In summer, spooling across the road dragging damp towels, bathing suits still wet and cold and sandy from the day before. A strange flat beach. Even when the tide was in, walking out and out to get waist deep. The tide rolling back out to reveal acres of wrinkled, suede-coloured sand, hard as wet concrete, water withdrawn to a distant line of smudged aquamarine on the far horizon. It wasn't always benign.

Staying out too long on one of the sandbanks, fingerlets of sandy water would begin gurgling into the suedette wrinkles. Shouts of Tide! Sudden trenches of deepening swirling water. Every summer at least one car would get caught on a sand bank. 'Lads' from the city careening in loops across the beach all afternoon. Before they realized it, tidal pools filling behind them. Us watching from the steps as water swirled around their stricken cars. Next day a man with a tractor would come and pull the ruined car to the slipway. A 'spring' tide brought blue water rushing up to the sea wall, smashing up and over, diamond showers crashing down again, again, again, wiping out beach and sand, leaving seawrack, planks, a palm tree, the head of a plastic doll. A reminder of the sea's power. Of its reach. Every summer brought a dead dog. Tossed over the seawall with a stone round its neck. The reek filling the steep cove down by the railway gates for days. There were flashers too. Old lads in battered raincoats, hiding in the bushes near the railway gates, whipping open coats to reveal a soft pink sausage hanging out of stained unbuttoned trousers. 'Don't stop or say anything,' Mum said, 'just run.' So we ran.

The best times of all were the holidays. A whole month in a rented house in Kerry, or Connemara, or West Cork, with Mum and Dad. Sometimes just a bungalow with rooms full of bunks, sometimes, gloriously, a proper house with its own gardens, a path to a lake, a tiny harbour, a rowing boat. Who is going to vow to swim every day no matter what the weather? Me, Dad, me! Cold wet togs pulled from a pile in the boot and dragged on with rain slashing across the chopped up water of the lake. Hot tea from the flask afterwards, cold sausages wrapped in greaseproof paper, a twist of salt. Sunburn in the evening after a day on the beach, Mum painting the little ones with Calamine lotion. The big ones looking beautiful, new clothes, tanned limbs, all smelling of Nivea. The hallway of the holiday rental gritty with sand, a jumble of metal buckets and spades, sandals, plastic cricket bat and wickets, fishing rods bought in the local village, a jar of bait, cries of: 'Anyone seen my jumper, t-shirt, blue cardi, black jeans, the baby's sun hat, the car keys, the picnic basket, the picnic rug, the Calamine lotion?' A cacophony rising to a crescendo as Dad says, 'Everyone in the car!' All cramming in. A trip planned the evening before to this beach, that cove, the 'bottomless' lake. The sea rough and salty, the waves thumping and dragging. The lakes brown and silky, the ground squishy underfoot, the water icy cold when you let your legs down out in the middle. Fishing trips in a hired boat. The water slap, slap, slapping the bow as the little outboard engine drives us forward into open sea. The engine stopping, fishing lines paid out over the side. The scream when you felt a jolt at the end of your line, the lure disappearing suddenly underwater. 'I've got one Dad!' Pulling in the line, the gleaming fish jumping and whirling, all muscle and swerve. Dad, or the fisherman, un-hooking it, handing it over, a flash of blood. Every so often a fish somersaulting free—Dad! The men taking the fish, bashing their heads against the seat, throwing them down onto the boards at the bottom of the boat where they thud and thump, going slower and slower, like clockwork winding down. 'More, Dad,' we shout like little savages. 'More!' Back at the house, my brother gutting the fish at the sink. The brilliant eyes now cloudy, slitting open soft silvery bellies, grey guts spilling out onto newspaper. Then onto the pan, hissing and spitting. From pan to plate, to be eaten straight away, with country butter, salt, new potatoes. 'Delicious!' go the big ones. I liked catching the fish but I didn't like eating them. They taste strange.

I wrote Dad a 'pome': '

1

Oh if you saw my Daddy
You would love him on the spot
He is brown and tall and very very nice
I'm sure you will be jealous to have a father like mine
But don't be a bit because you have your own
I rather my father than any other man in the world
He has lovely blue eyes and his hair isn't curled

2

These verses are longer than 'Uimhir a h-Aon'
You understand Irish oh yes I forgot you do
It is very nice isn't it you know that's quite true
I love Irish but I rather Daddy
I suppose all sensible people do!!
Daddy is nice nobody nicer
You can have your opinion too

3

Daddy is nice Mummy is nice
They are both such darlings I don't know how to think
But there's one thing I'll always do
I'll always stay true to them to Daddy
Daddy's like honey and sugar what else so sweet
And if you have a father as nice as mine
I bet ten pounds that you haven't
So again you will have to take your choice

4

I love Daddy I hope he likes me
Because Daddy's the nicest friend you could have
I cannot think what to write about
So this is the end of my roundabout.

Then it was the last summer before catastrophe struck. The sun shining. The doors and windows of the house standing open night and day. All of us in the garden. Dad dressed in linen, festooned with tanned children. Mum, standing apart, holding my younger, delicate sister in her arms, looking angry. Defiant. Alone.

4

A wealthy relative of Mum's died and left his entire swag to the Archbishop of Dublin. The *Archbishop*. Alone in his vast palace overlooking the sea, dressed in silks, linens, lace, satin brocades, driven everywhere in chauffeured limousines, eating the finest food, sleeping on embroidered embossed sheets.

Mum decided to write to him.

No reply.

Then, a stormy black-as-pitch night, wind buffeting squalls of rain in off the sea, a loud knocking on the front door, the door almost blown in, and Mum sees a young priest. He pushed an envelope into her hand: 'From the Archbishop.'

Inside were three hundred pounds. A drop, without explanation, from Your Lordship's ocean.

Mum said: 'This will send the twins to boarding school.'

Our trunks were bought. Lists were filled: one navy Sunday dress with detachable white collars. Two everyday skirts. One blue jumper. One navy divided skirt. Two pairs navy over knickers. Two pairs white under knickers. One flannel. One toothbrush. And on and on, the lists pinned to the insides of the trunk.

For the week before we went, my head rang. Trapped in an unreality I couldn't get out of.

Mum and Dad drove us down, but Mum was so withdrawn I don't remember her hugging us goodbye. A grey yard. A massive four-storey grey barracks, more prison than school. Our trunks taken out of the boot, a hug from Dad, and then the family car swinging around the corner and down the avenue was gone.

A nun, took me by the hand, walked me, without Twin Sister, down a long, faux marble floored corridor, my new leather shoes loud on the harsh floor.

When I emerged, seven years later, I was a different person: bumptious on the outside, frozen on the inside. Divided, as R. D. Laing, would say, from my Real Self.

One night I sat out on a windowsill in the dark in my nightdress. If I got pneumonia, surely that would get me home? Did Twin Sister not want to run away too? 'Don't be stupid. What would we do once we got outside the gates?'

In this new world Twin Sister and I drifted apart. One night I whispered to her, horrified: men have to put their thing inside women to make babies! Yes, she said, coolly. She already knew that.

She knew, and hadn't told me? I felt ridiculous. And even more alone.

By the standards of the horrors going on in other institutions, like the 'Mother and Baby Homes', we Sacred Heart girls led privileged lives. As in all institutions though—prisons, boarding schools, old people's homes, lunatic asylums—the rule was the same: you adapt or you go under. In order to survive you must 'entomb' your real self. A self you may never be able to retrieve.

Make an adaptation that will probably scar you for life.

Love was banished. 'Self-love is no love,' was the nuns' mantra. The only love allowed was love of Jesus. And God. And the Virgin Mary, with heavy emphasis on virgin. Along with love, sensuality was banished. Kissing in films, girls dancing together at evening 'rec,' the reading of girl mags smuggled in by the day boarders, all were ferociously stamped down on by the celibate nuns, most of whom had entered the convent in their teens and had to stamp down ferociously on their own feelings.

Trapped in a horribly distorted system, they tried to trap us too.

5

Back at home, without our knowing, something far more terrible was taking place. My younger sister Cathy's delicate health had deteriorated catastrophically. Days shy of her seveneth birthday, she died.

Twin Sister and I were told of her death in the lunch file. 'Your sister Cathy died this morning.' We weren't told what had happened, we weren't comforted, we weren't given the opportunity to ring home. It was just, here's the news, now get on to Maths class. I don't even remember there being a discussion about allowing us home for the funeral.

Four weeks later, we arrived back to a household in deep shock. Strangers to ourselves at school, now we were strangers at home.

6

'Yes,' Mum was saying, 'but why did God have to take *my* child?'

I felt irritated. Not *that* again.

But of course it was *that* again.

Cathy.

Underneath everything that had been joyful and normal and big happy family in 'Seabank,' the abnormal had ticked away like a time-bomb: Cathy's health.

Born with a hole in her heart, Cathy was a 'blue baby.' These days, thanks to a brilliant female surgeon, 'blue babies' can be operated on, the hole stitched up, their fatal lack of oxygen mended. In Cathy's day it was a death sentence.

Mum said the doctors would say to her and Dad, 'Just try to keep her alive. We'll find a cure.' They probably meant to be kind. But it seemed unutterably cruel. How could Mum, or Dad, parents to eight other children, keep their adored, mortally injured little 'blue' baby alive when all the medics in the world couldn't?

Cathy developed a cerebral abscess. A family friend, a former matron, advised Mum and Dad an operation was the only hope. It offered no certainty, but with death an absolute certainty, it was all there was.

The night before Cathy was due to be operated on, Dad lost his nerve. He didn't, couldn't go in to the hospital to be with Cathy and Mum. Mum was left on her own with her adored little daughter, her little head shaved for next day's operation on her brain, that might, or might not work.

How frightened they both must have been. How alone.

Cathy didn't survive the operation.

Mum and Dad's relationship didn't survive her death.

Cathy's death shattered everything. We went from Mum, Dad, a sprawling brood in a lovely old house by the sea, with its beautiful garden and orchard, ponies in the garage, peaches and roses and summers in the garden, down to two shattered adults, cardboard cut-out figures, each alone inside their agony, unable to help each other. Or to help us.

We went from technicolour to black and white. From warmth and sunshine, from dinner parties and children's parties, from starched and ironed pink cotton summer uniforms, from Dad's corn-on-the-cob pulled from the garden and eaten hot, butter dribbling down between our fingers in front of a blazing fire in the drawing room, from pungent roses with petals soft as baby skin, to slamming doors, ashes piled in a cold grate, the Big Ones telling us Younger Ones to shut up. To Go and Find Something To Do. To, FOR GOD'S SAKE BE QUIET AND STOP ANNOYING EVERYONE.

From heaven to hell.

Mum went to bed, lying in a blacked-out bedroom, curtains drawn, day after day. Everyone was told to GO AWAY. No, she did not want anything. She particularly did not want Dad. There was no counselling. Not for Mum, or Dad, not for any of us. No sharing of information, what had happened, how it had happened, why. For us younger ones it was: why couldn't Mum get out of bed, pull the curtains, brush her hair, put some clothes on, come downstairs and make everything normal again?

We turned to Dad. Help us, Dad. Comfort us, Dad. Tell us Mum is a bad, bad person.

Mum said 'all these people' told her she had her other children, she should love them. But, Mum said, she 'didn't want' her other children. She wanted Cathy. At the time we took it as evidence of Mum's hideousness. Nobody thought to tell us that traumatised and grief-stricken, she could find little solace in us, her living children. Of course she wanted Cathy.

Mum, in grief freefall, rejected us. So we rejected her. And she was left alone to carry the terrible, life-destroying agony of losing her beautiful little daughter, dry-eyed and alone in the midst of a big noisy family who thought she was a terrible human being.

Soon after Cathy's death, Dad insisted that 'Seabank' be sold. Mum did everything she could to dissuade him. 'Seabank' had been a gift from her godmother to her. Mum should have been able to say NO to Dad. To feck off. But in those days even good men like Dad had the power to insist. He said he couldn't bear living there any longer because of all the memories.

'Memories are all we've got!' Mum cried.

'Seabank' was put up for sale. Tea chests, still scented with fragrant tea leaves rustling in their silvery insides arrived, followed by men in white coats who packed and packed. A huge van pulled into the drive. And we moved to a redbrick house where the earth smelled of dog shit and you couldn't even see the sea, never mind hear or smell it.

The ponies, the beautiful garden, the peaches hot from the sun, the greenhouse, Twin Sister and I's bedroom in the attic, the sea, the beach, the ice cream wafers from the Tower shop, the drawing room with its big rattling windows looking down onto the garden and the greengage tree—all were gone.

Far from improving Mum's health, she was more alienated, more withdrawn, more angry than ever.

Go *Away*.

Everyone longed for her return. When she sat like a ghost at the dinner table, and someone—maybe Dad?—told a joke and Mum looked up for a minute, gave the smallest laugh, the whole table erupted: Ha!Ha!Ha!Ha!Ha!

Such relief! Mum hasn't totally rejected us all! Mum doesn't 10,000% hate life! Mum doesn't 10,000% hate Dad!

We didn't notice that Mum had stopped smiling long before we stopped shrieking.

17

7

Bills piled up, unopened on Dad's desk. Mum said, 'Go in there and sort them *out.'* Dad said tidying his desk gave him asthma. *All that dust.* Mum said there wouldn't *be* dust if he kept it tidy. If he paid the bills when they came in.

Dad was hopeless with money. Brought up in great privilege in 'Derrybawn,' it was never the value of the beautiful house and lands, the river, the woodlands, the lush fields, that mattered to him. It was the feelings attached to those places, to the rivers, the lands, to the people who lived there.

The big houses—'Phoenix Hill,' 'Derrybawn,' 'Seabank,' 24 Fitzwilliam Square— all now worth millions, were sold off for a pittance one by one, while our financial fortunes stayed at rocky bottom.

Everything was done on a shoestring. Riding hats, jackets, white blouses and jodhpurs for gymkhanas and hunts were hand-me-downs. Boarding school uniforms were 'turned' —oh the *shame*—for a second year's wear. Party dresses were home-made or hand-me-downs from 'the others.' Tennis was practised with old heavy rackets and soggy balls up against the garage doors. Ponies were Connemaras Dad bought at the Clifden Horse Fair. Or through someone he'd done a favour for in the Land Commission.

We never achieved the sleek, blonde, bulletproof confidence of the fully moneyed 'poshies.' We were too many, too rackety, too poor, to really pass muster.

But there was a record player and stacks of Dad's wonderful 78s. The bookshelves in the drawing room held Alice in Wonderland. Black Beauty. Christopher Robin. Robinson Crusoe. The Red Badge of Courage. Wuthering Heights. Pride and Prejudice. Madame Bovary, Brighton Rock, The Power and the Glory, The End of the

Affair, Tess of the d'Urbervilles, Lord Jim, Heart of Darkness, The Hound of the Baskervilles, Vile Bodies, The Third Policeman, The Old Man and the Sea, The Prime of Miss Jean Brodie, One Day in the Life of Ivan Denisovich, War and Peace, Anna Karenina. Crime and Punishment.

I don't remember ever being told *not* to read a book.

8

There was one last family holiday together. Probably the best holiday of all. Big Sister, now living in London, invited her flatmate, Hattie Waugh, daughter of the famous Evelyn, and Tom Benson, then the hottest chef in London, at Parkes Restaurant in Knightsbridge, then the hottest eatery in London, to join us.

Like all big families, our behaviour improved dramatically with visitors around. Hattie and Tom were a delightful audience. We performed happy family while they cheered us on. Tom, working class from Liverpool, jumped out of bed every morning eager to drink in more of this nectar. He brought wine and flowers for Mum, an entire Stilton for Dad. For Twin Sister and me, he brought blue Bob Dylan hats. Dad, who adored Evelyn Waugh, wrote a poem for Hattie.

For Hatty Waugh
Young woman!' do you know the riches you possess,
The visions you may see and pass them by?
You can look on them later for they grow no less
And see them brighter with your inward eye.

Hattie said Mum she was the most feminine woman she had ever seen.

One evening Tom took Mum and Dad, Hattie and the older ones out to dinner. In those days that meant a hotel restaurant. When the—very expensive—red wine Tom had ordered arrived, it was cold. Shocked, Tom sent it back, explaining it should be *chambre*. A suspiciously few minutes later, the young country girl waitress came back with a *very* warm bottle.

'What did you do to it?' Tom asked.

'We *boyled* it,' was the never to be forgotten reply.

A holiday house by the sea had been found. A chalet. The sea, the brightest blue, swelled and rolled in every window. The sun danced across its sparkling surface as we raced down the beach to throw ourselves in.

One afternoon a whitebait shoal came in, the water suddenly a heaving boiling mass of tiny silver bodies followed by hundreds of mackerel. Urged on by Dad, trousers pulled up to his knees, and Tom, tight white jeans soaked to the waist, we ran up and down to the house with colanders, fishing nets, sieves, saucepans, basins. Anything to catch the bounty in.

That night's supper was whitebait and fillet of mackerel rolled in seasoned flour, served with homemade mayonnaise and new potatoes. Prepared and cooked by Tom.

Everyone high, sunburnt, happy. Even Mum happy.

I saw London Sister, a sun-browned Madonna standing in the corner, as if she had brought this entire miracle about.

In a way she had.

9

At last came the time to leave school.

At home life was grim. One by one the big ones left. Empty rooms, hollow passages. Dad, home from the office, would go straight upstairs to bed. Mum alone in the drawing room with a fire that wouldn't have heated a mouse, with her books from the RDS, her little dog at her feet, her knitting.

Unhappiness everywhere.

One morning I came into the kitchen. Mum was at the cooker, angled and angry, Dad at the table, a hollowed-out skeleton.

'So,' Mum was saying, turned towards Dad, 'do you want this porridge or not?' She banged a wooden spoon. The porridge, like stiffening concrete, fell into a bowl. Dad just managed a *Yes*. Mum shoved the bowl down the table towards him.

Splashing in some cold milk, Dad attempted to eat.

Next, Mum was holding up a boiled egg. The egg had cracked in the saucepan. A thick rubbery frill, rimed with scum, extruded from the shell. Mum dumped the egg into a chipped, blue and white-striped egg cup and sent it down the table after the porridge. Dad looked up, made a sound somewhere between a groan and a strangled scream, his chair legs squealing on the tiled floor as he pushed it back. Mum watched. If he'd slammed the door it might have been better, but he just let it click to behind him. Mum, looking as if her bones might snap out of their sockets, clattered everything—dishes, saucepan, hideous boiled egg, plate of uneaten porridge—into the sink.

Seeing me watching she turned and snarled: 'So what are you standing there for?'

I was sitting upstairs on Mum's bed talking to Dad. Outside it was dark, the dark black cold marshalled at the big window. 'I'll pull the curtains,' I said to Dad. 'Why don't I go get you a hot bottle?' Would you like an omelette? I could make you a hot whiskey, wouldn't that be nice?'

Dad sitting up, a bank of flattened thin pillows awkwardly

stacked behind him, a book about Joan of Arc in French, Bien-heureuse Jeanne d'Arc, open on his lap, its thick art paper pages with uncut edges untouched, shook his head.

'Are you SURE you wouldn't like a hot toddy?' I said. 'I know there's a drop left in the bottle. It would only take me a minute.'

In a sudden silence, he looked across at me, his eyes huge: 'I don't believe in anything anymore.' He said it so quietly I barely heard. His fingers touched the book's opened pages, 'Not *anything*.'

My heart began a panic-stricken pounding. 'I'm going to go and make some tea.' Afraid to even look at Dad as I walked around the end of his bed, I grasped open the door, muttered *'Tea.'* Ran.

I ran down the stairs so fast Mum called out, 'What's happening? What's the matter?' But I didn't reply. I couldn't.

What's the *matter* with Dad? I asked the big ones when they came home. Why is he so ill? Why can't the doctor *DO* something?

Second Oldest sister said: 'Nothing is *the matter*. Why don't you get a job and stop worrying them both to death?'

'What is *wrong* though?.

'There's nothing *wrong*.' Second Eldest Sister said, 'Why do you always have to be so bloody dramatic?'

'Why are you always so interfering?' Mum said.

The doctor said: 'Your father probably shouldn't push the boat too far out from shore. You know? His days of going off to rugby matches and cheering from the stands are probably over!' He laughed a big, pipe-smoking, tweed jacket wearing, doctor laugh. I stared at him. I knew he was a kind man. But what did he MEAN? Had Dad ever even been to a rugby match?

Second Eldest sister decided to go volunteering in Africa. I saw her and Dad standing on the landing outside the drawing room. The same height. Tall and thin, their heads close. Like lovers. Saying

22

goodbye. Lovers who know they will never see each other again.
My heart thrashing, I ran back downstairs.

Then it was just Mum, Dad, me, and the two littles. The house getting sadder and sadder. Dustier. More uncared for.

Third Eldest Sister came home for holidays from her nursing training. She started cleaning the kitchen. Scraping off inch thick grime. 'I'll make this place *shine,*' she said, her own face shining. But then she had to go back to college. A deep ochre high-tide mark showed where she'd had to give up.

London Sister rang. She was working for Peter Benenson, the founder of Amnesty International. There was a job for a junior secretary-cum-receptionist. Would I like to come over? Yes, I said, not thinking twice. *Yes.*

I found a poem Dad had written in those last days:

The Weaver's Hands are Tied
The Speaker's voice is still
No longer possible the cry of full felt pain
Or the winner's arrogant shout of victory
Only a faint whimper of self pity
From a desert of his own making.
No! Hands tied, voice stilled,
I wait among the valley fields
Listening for the sound of a horn from the hills
Call me home.

So unbearably alone.

10

In London I moved in with London Sister.

At home us younger ones used to laugh at London Sister. Mum had dispatched her, aged 10, to her very posh alma mater, 'New Hall,' built on the footprint of Henry VIII's first palace in 1517. Sent off in a man's camel coat, cinched around the waist with one of Dad's leather belts, a suitcase held together with a strap, London Sister said she almost died of shame. She came back with a posh accent. Sang 'Ding Dong Merrily on High' at Christmas, and talked about 'the Arrish.'

We thought she was mad. We had to be careful though. She went actually mad if things didn't go the way she wanted: 'Why can't we do it the *nice* way?' We'd laugh, then scatter, as she roared up the passage, crimson faced, wielding the sweeping brush.

Now PA to Peter Benenson, in Amnesty in London, she was Miss Perfect Private Secretary. She never over-ate. Or over-drank. She brushed her teeth for ten minutes every night. She made her own clothes, not my type of sewing, lashing something together in a couple of hours, but beautifully finished dresses with gussets and darts and invisible hemming, tweed jackets with lining, pockets, collars. She hung her clothes on hangers, folded her sweaters, laying tissue paper in between. She bought hardback books. Carried Ted Hughes's The Hawk in the Rain on the Tube.

She had ardent admirers. Fruity, upper class 'Simons' and 'Olivers' with good hair and three-piece suits. They took her to expensive restaurants, to the opera, the ballet, the theatre, to country house weekends.

Critically, they worshipped.

I worshipped too. Trotting eagerly—a shaggy, chattering, mountain pony—alongside a gleaming thoroughbred.

PART TWO

'The devil doesn't come dressed in a red cape and pointy horns. He comes as everything you've ever wished for.'

Tucker Max, *Assholes Finish First*

1

It was London Sister who brought 'him,' and his friend, to our house. Dad was in hospital so the two men sat at Dad's end of the dinner table; Mum, at the other end, looked furious: what was London Sister *thinking*, 'bringing men like that' into the house.

Men like what?

Flying in from Africa, 'they were in a bad way.' Booted out by their wives for bad behaviour, London Sister and her friend had been asked to rescue them. They'd decided to bring them over to Ireland. Get their minds off domestic woes.

London Sister was clearly already in love with the handsome Clint Eastwood lookalike from then Rhodesia. He brought wine and flowers for Mum. Talked to 'the littles.' Sweetly smiled.

The other one was silent. Brooding. Film star beautiful. Large lustrous brown eyes, thick black hair in a Beatles' mop, tanned, tall, skinny, long-fingered tan hands. The enormous eyes fastened on me as I got up to fetch gravy off the sideboard, burned through my green tweed miniskirt, feasted on my bum. Tripping on the dining room rug, cheeks on fire, I almost dropped the gravy boat. Mum looked quickly at him. Quickly at me. 'Put that down there.'

How my 17-year-old heart pounded!

Later, leaving, alone suddenly in the hall, he glanced up from under that hair. Eyes almost black in the dim hall light: *Yes,* those eyes said, he knew exactly how shit the world was. What he *needed*, he said, eyes locking on, dismissing the entire evening and everyone in it, was a cold beer.

I catapulted head first down love's helter skelter.

I had found my Heathcliff.

Back in London, London Sister and the handsome Clint Eastwood lookalike moved in together.

Their liaison had to be kept secret from Dad. Horrified that his eldest daughter, noted for serious Blessed Virgin Mary vibes, was even contemplating life with a MARRIED MAN, Dad would have lost his mind if he'd known she was having the best sex of her life with the same guy. Day and night. As often as possible in between.

It was decided London Sister would get her lover's marriage annulled. So that she and he could have their love, their ardent fucking, blessed by Mother Church. And by Dad.

Looking beautiful—sky-blue scarf knotted Aubrey Hepburn style, modest linen dress, exquisite black pumps, the picture of film starry innocence—London Sister tripped off every other day to Brompton Oratory to plead with the good Jesuits to intervene with the Holy Father—the Pope no less!—to have her man's marriage, which she assured us all was a horribly, desperately unhappy one, scrubbed from the record.

The Jesuits got enthusiastically stuck in. Sis was assigned a Personal Confessor. Weekly updates on the progress of the annulment were sent over to Ireland while the star-crossed lovers went at it hammer and tongs in the bedroom.

An annulment is a fantastical piece of Jesuitical jiggery pokery. Bypassing then adamantine Catholic strictures against divorce, it annuls the original marriage on four grounds: 'defect of form,' 'defect of contract' defect of will,' 'defect of capacity', that is, you weren't both Catholic. You weren't fully behind the Till Death Do us Part bit. You were bonkers. You were already married to a Prod.

Hey Presto! Your marriage was disappeared! It took years, went through endless Papal courts, involved endless mental gymnastics, and cost thousands.

The best kind of Catholicism, right?

In the end I think London Sister and her man got bored. One

sunny day they rang their friends, filled the bath with ice and champagne, walked down to the local registry office, and tied the knot.

Dad was thoroughly taken aback. I think Mum suspected all along the Jesuitical fol de rol was to impress Dad. We younger ones thought it sensationally romantic. He adored her. She adored being adored. They had to fight to get their love recognised! Hurrahs!

In London they were part of the posh boys club then involved in development in Africa. The brightest of bright scholars from Oxbridge advising Ministers in the newly independent states: Zimbabwe, Kenya, Zambia, Botswana. Democracies so young that access to Presidents, Ministers for Finance, Ministers for Development, was easy. These clever boys wrote for the FT. Influenced African governments policies. Set up schools in mountain villages.

Africa was shaking off the shackles of colonialism! They were there to help! And have a terrific time in the process.

In visits to London they got together, exotic as the Bloomsbury Set. Clever, and beautiful. They attended plays by Athol Fugard. Went to the Ritz for dinner with the Minister of Finance from Zambia. One was a muse for Lucien Freud. I watched from the sidelines, agog.

Film star man, now back with his wife, was part of 'the set.' I babysat for them, their pretty mop-haired children, side by side on the spare mattress on the floor. He drove me home, eyeing up my miniskirt. But didn't pay me my babysitter fee. Cheapskate! I was too young, too shy, to insist.

2

In London for a weekend, at London Sister's invitation, to get over a broken heart, film star man was also there, also staying at London

Sister's flat. Also nursing a broken heart. His beautiful wife had rung him from Africa three nights before to say she was marrying his 'best' friend. He was in Rome when he got the call. He and another, better, best friend got sensationally drunk and trashed their hotel room. I thought it the most rock and roll thing I'd ever heard: television sets flying out through long Roman windows smashing onto cobbled streets below. Antique mirrors shattering onto parquet floors. Crackled Victorian hand basins ripped from walls, water rushing from ancient brass faucets.

How were they not arrested?

London Sister said it was a very exclusive hotel. It wouldn't have been the first time something like that had happened. Rock stars, etc. If you paid up, tipped heavily, that would be the end of it.

What? but she was already in her bedroom getting dressed. We'd been invited out to Parkes, Tom Benson's restaurant in Knightsbridge. Film star man was invited along too. They could hardly leave him alone in the flat with his broken heart, could they?

He stared at me all night. Huge burning eyes. Isolating me. Catching me in the spotlight of his desire, everyone and everything else blurring into the background. London Sister glanced across between mouthfuls. Brother-in-Law smiled down at his plate. Velvety wine was poured into the biggest, thinnest glasses. White oval plates were carried in exuding auras of fragrant steam. 'Poached sweetbreads with grilled asparagus.' 'Hen Turkey cooked in Red Wine with Black Cherries.' 'Boeuf en Croute with potatoes Dauphinoise.' 'Spring greens poached in jus de poule.' Each forkful an orgasm in the mouth.

Tom appeared, hot and shiny faced after hours in the kitchen, ordering up more wine, asking how the food was, wondered why we were all so bloody *QUIET*.

Back at London Sister's flat, Brother-in-Law said it would be silly for film star man to sleep on the two-seater sofa, *So bloody uncomfortable*. Why didn't he take the spare single bed in the room where I was? 'And no funny business, okay?' he said, carrying in blankets and sheets, a lumpy cushion in a pillow case.

I heard film star man brushing his teeth in the bathroom. The bedroom door clicking open, his body sliding into the other bed. Silence.

Next thing, film star man was up. Leanly naked apart from a pair of striped jocks, long legs going past the end of my bed, 'Mind if I close these curtains a bit? That street lamp is very bright?' I'm about to say yes but he's already doing it. Then he was standing beside my bed, just visible in the near dark: 'Mind if I get in for a bit?' Again, before the question could be answered, he was in. Long, lean, vigorous. 'Ooooh, that's better,' arms and legs wrapped around me. 'C'mere.' I played it cool. As if having a globe-trotting, older, married Don Juan entering my bed was an everyday, every night occurrence. Next thing, with a delighted gasp, he was inside me.

Me play hot Lolita to your James Bond! Again! Again! Faking noisy delight.

Finally he rolled off: 'You're *fantastic*.' He leaned on his elbows. Looked down. I giggled. Thrilled with myself. My performance.

In the morning, London Sister knew immediately. Stomping round the flat on stiff legs, wet hair up in a turban, her *How-CouldYou?* face on. Brother-in-Law was also displeased: I had made the Queen cross. *HowDareI?*

What did I care? I was in love!

Slamming out the door, London Sister was gone, her man hurrying out after her.

I ran a bath.

I'm in a film! Running a bath for my lover! Steam rushed up the windows, covering the mirror over the handbasin. I held over-flowing capfuls of London Sister's expensive bubble bath under the gushing tap.

I ran back to the bedroom, 'I've run us a bath!' Meaning: Come play film stars in my scented paradise!

Film star man, now on the spare bed, is lying on his back.

Laughing, I run back into the bathroom, scoop up a tooth mug full of mountaining bubbles. Back in the bedroom I flick drops of fragrant frothiness towards his face. He shoots upright. White faced. Furious. 'That went into my fucking *ear.*'

I am too shocked to move.

Back in the bathroom, bubbles disappearing in cooling water, I lock the door.

Fuck *you.*

'Let me in! Don't be daft! Open up!' The door handle rattles.

'You look like an angry toddler!' he says, squeezing in behind me. Then, 'I was *joking* silly!' then, 'Come *on.'*

He promises breakfast in a fancy hotel in town. A boat on the river. A visit to Biba's. A visit to an art gallery. Whatever I want.

James Bond dangling treats. James Bond whistling. Wagging my tail, I ran after him.

3

We went to Belfast. He 'couldn't bear to let go,' he said. 'You're the best thing that ever happened to me.' We fucked till my skin sang. We walked around the city, two as one, everyone smiling at love.

On Monday I got the train home. My brother was waiting at the station. My brother never met me off anything, anywhere, but I was so buzzing from all the fucking and drinking and eating and this gorgeous adult man all over me, saying he loved me, saying I must come and live with him, now immediately, *today,* that he'd never met anyone like me ever, ever before, that we'd find a way, that *he'd* find a way, that it wasn't until I got into the car with my brother, and he said, smirking a little as he bent forward to put the key into the ignition, 'Well you're in for it,' that I started to feel alarmed. Why *had* he come? How did he know to come to this station? This train?

Mum was waiting behind the hall door, icily furious. 'Your father is upstairs.' I looked around, 'What—?'

'*Now,*' Mum said, pointing at the stairs.

Dad pushed himself up and back in the bed as I came round the door. 'My dear child—'

I sat on Mum's bed, suddenly aware of my heart beat-beating.

'Your sister rang—' Dad began.

'What—?' but Dad held up a hand.

'She's told me everything.' His hand fell back onto the folded-down sheet. 'What in the name of God were you thinking child? This married man. This philanderer. This *known* philanderer.'

Dad stared at me, his eyes the bluest blue.

'His wife has *left* him, Dad.'

'Good God, child,' Dad exclaimed.

'She's married his best friend,' I said, 'she's *gone.*'

Dad clapped a hand to his high, wrinkled forehead, 'Oh my God.' Then, 'What kind of people are these?'

'He *loves* me, Dad.'

'He has no right to love anyone!' Dad shouted, 'he's a *married* man.'

'And he's old enough to be your father. 'And he's a notorious—'

'*Dad.*'

33

'Your sister tells me he's been carrying on affairs while he and his wife were still together.

'I *love* him, Dad.'

Dad went quiet. 'This is much, much worse than I thought,' he said.

Finally he told me to call Mum. 'She's to go to her room,' he said, 'and stay there. No one is to talk to her. Or have anything to do with her. Until I decide what to do. Her meals will be brought up on a tray.'

'This way,' Mum said, holding the door. Colder than a Nazi gaoler. The younger ones down in the hall stared up as Mum walked me down the stairs, across the landing and into my room. Her hand on the door handle, she said, 'Go in there and stay in there until you are told to come out.'

As if I were a dog.

Later I heard supper being prepared. Onion frying. The radio on. The younger ones muffled voices. I was in too much shock to cry.

I lay on my bed watching evening, then night, taking over the garden, the trees, the swing. Dark pouring down from a black sky.

The next morning Dad was up and dressed in his court suit. He and Mum were waiting for me in the dining room. I felt as if I'd been ill: faint, unsure.

'Your mother and I have an appointment with Tom,' Dad said.

'What?'

Dad picked his leather gloves up off the sideboard. 'Your mother and I are going to discuss this case with him. We will see you later.'

They must have forgotten to order me back to my room because I went down to the kitchen where I could hear my brother.

'What are Mum and Dad *doing*?'

'They're making you a Ward of Court,' my brother said, piling jam onto a generously buttered piece of toast.

"What's a Ward of Court?' I held onto the back of one of the kitchen chairs.

'It puts you under the control of the Court,' my brother said, pouring tea. They do it for *amadáns*,' he said grinning, 'for crazy people.'

'What?'

'What did you think was going to happen?' he said, spooning sugar into his tea. 'That they would welcome you with open arms!? You and your Don Juan?'

I was in the garden, clumsily clasping the dog who was wriggling and didn't want to be clasped, when the kitchen door opened. Mum, her coat still on, said, 'Who said you could come out of your room?' She held the door. 'Get back up those stairs immediately. And leave the dog where she is.'

She said something as I ran past, but I couldn't hear through the blood thundering in my ears.

The meeting with Dad's barrister friend had had to be delayed. He was involved in a big case. On Friday Mum called up the stairs: 'There's a telegram for you.'

Mum on one side, Dad dressed for the office on the other, they watched as I read, the words blurring as I went: 'BBC OFFER YOU PLACE ON GRACE WYNDHAM GOLDIE TV COURSE STOP STARTING TUESDAY 12 JUNE STOP PLEASE CONFIRM ATTEND-ANCE ASAP STOP.'

My hand shaking, I looked up at Mum. Then at Dad. 'I've been offered a place on the Grace Wyndham course at the BBC,' I said, handing over the telegram.

That evening I'm called to the drawing room. Mum is in her chair by the fire. Dad in his. Dad is holding the telegram. 'Your

Mother and I have decided this is too important an opportunity for you to miss.' My heart begins: pit a pat, pit a pat. 'But you go on ONE condition,' Dad continues, 'you are never, *ever* to see this man again. Is that clear? You will stay with your sister and she—' I don't remember anymore, just me saying, 'I promise, I *PROMISE*, Dad.'

Dad said my sister and her husband had 'very kindly' agreed to give me her spare room. I was to write home every week. And I was never EVER to put my family through something like this ever again.

I *promise.*

I was allowed come downstairs.

I think Mum knew, before I did, what was going to happen. But I was on a plane, high above clouds packed tight as folded lint over Dublin Bay, the sea appearing and disappearing as the plane banked steeply, climbing up, up, and away, carrying me to London.

London Sister stared when I said I was going out for a walk. At nine o'clock at night? I was going to tell her the truth, that I was going to meet 'him,' to tell him I couldn't move in with him, that I'd swear-promised Dad I would never see him again. But she'd gone over to the sink and started washing up. As if I'd already left.

Okay, and fuck you too.

He was waiting in the pub. He seemed different. He was wearing a suit. Less Don Juan, more just another Englishman in a pub in London.

I'd barely sat down before he started: you either move in with me now, or you can forget about it. I'm not hanging around for you to make up your mind. For your bloody father to stop being so bloody hysterical.

Afterwards, as we said goodbye around the corner from my sister's, he said, 'You've got twenty-four hours to make up your mind.'

In their bathroom I tried to cover the hickies on my neck with her concealer. Then sitting around the table, drinking tea, I went into super jolly mode, the BBC course, how FANTASTIC it was going to be.

Diversionary tactics.

Two days later he was waiting outside BBC Television Centre in a pillarbox red Deux Chevaux with canvas seats. He laughed at the amount I kissed him. 'Steady on. You'll have us done for indecency.' I wanted to be the most indecent Lolita in the world.

On the final day of the course, an Irish guy and I did Molly Bloom's soliloquy from Ulysses as our signing off piece. He directed while I read, a white towel shawled around my shoulders. Everyone clapped and said it was terrific. But when I saw it played back in the editing suite I thought I looked, and sounded, like the inexperienced schoolgirl I really was.

4

London Sister was tight-lipped as I dragged my case across the floor. 'You're putting her in a very awkward position,' Brother-in-Law said. I knew I was. I didn't want to. But I wanted Film Star man more.

They didn't come to the door to say goodbye.

The BBC offered a job. A lowly secretarial one, but in White City. A tall woman in grey cardigan, grey skirt, long, serious, horse face, showed me a sheet with all the grades I could work up through to become a PA. 'Approximately seven years,' she said, 'depending on your diligence.' She reminded me of the nuns. People who made everything, even beautiful things, seem ugly.

J. had rented a modern bedsit with a single bed in newly built flats off Hampstead. A tiny kitchen. A tinier bathroom. He wanted to fuck all night and get up at 7 in the morning. 'Africa time!' he said. I felt chewed. Dazed.

A friend said a filmmaker could offer a room in his house just off Kensington Gardens. Most of the time, he said, the filmmaker would be away, in Africa filming, or in France with his new French wife.

Yes please. J. was thrilled. It was free, and beautiful, and right beside Kensington Gardens.

Our life together started.

We started with sex. Then J. running down to the kitchen coming back up with tea. Sitting up in bed, smoking Gauloises, drinking tea, J. laughing at my impersonations of the horse faced lady in the BBC, Richrd Dimbleby combing his hair in the studio. Telling him the only thing anyone ever got fired at the BBC for was for pissing down the lift shaft. *I know!*

Up and into one's teenage finery and across the park, with weekend Londoners flying kites, sailing model yachts on the ponds, J. pointing out the Henry Moore, the sundial, how to read it. Beer and toasted cheese by the river. A visit to J.'s friends from South Africa. Former members of the ANC. Jewish and cheerful, a packed house with drinks and daughters, every surface covered with books. J's. grown-up world. I felt young and irrelevant.

Off to late-night cinema. The latest James Bond, faces like white flowers in the dark. Imagine living like this? This fast? This sexily?

Afterwards, walking home: 'Do you love me more than anyone in the whole world, do you?' J. laughing, saying, 'Of course!' 'Definitely definitely definitely?' J. laughing, 'Definitely.'

I want to eat you. You can eat my bum. Yum yum yum yum! J.stop! People are looking. Fuck people. No fuck me. Here? Okay.

J. *stop*. You'll get us arrested!

Then J., not working. Somehow not part of 'the clever set' anymore. His friend, who had gone off with his wife, was a key member; J. being there was awkward. One morning the divorce papers arrived. 'Decree Nisi,' said J.

'It sounds like a disease,' I laughed. But J. didn't laugh.

His first wife, in absence, became ever more beautiful: 'Fantastic hair.' More clever: 'She got straight A's at the LSE.' More innovative: 'She always had a solution! Even when we didn't have a brass farthing! She used boot polish as eyeliner!'

I crept downstairs with my mousy hair, my ridiculous Leaving Certificate, my spectacular absence of accomplishment in the innovations department.

J. spent days in bed.

Ready for work, I stood at the bedroom door. 'Goodbye so?' 'G'bye.' 'I'll see you this evening?' 'You will.' 'Will we go out and do something?' 'No.' 'Why not?' 'Because I don't want to.' 'What about me?' 'What about you?'

Trying another tack: 'What do you think of my new dress from Shepherd's Bush Market?' 'It's okay.' Twirling around, 'Does my bum look big?' 'Enormous.'

Out the door then, crushed. Eating two donuts in the canteen, too much lunch, plus cakes at tea. If my bum is enormous, why not?

Back home after six. J. still in bed. He's reading. Would he like a drink? No. Would he like supper? No. Would he like a slap on the belly with a wet fish? Haha, very funny.

Downstairs for more eating. Standing in front of the fridge stuffing in slices of ham, leftover shepherd's pie, lumps of feta floating in a jar of olive oil. All swilled down with mouthfuls of wine from the bottle in the fridge door.

J. appears unexpectedly. Looking disgusted he leans in and takes out a beer. Leaves again. Without a word.

Tipsy now, wobbling with self-hatred, I go upstairs and stand by the bed. 'Why won't you talk to me J., *why?*' 'I'm reading.' 'Can you stop reading for a minute and talk? Please?' 'No.' *'Please!'* 'No.' 'Why not?' 'Because I don't fucking want to.' 'But why?' 'That's why. Now fuck off.'

Downstairs for more wine. More slices of ham. A Gauloise. Another Gauloise. Another glass of wine. Another—

Back upstairs. The bedroom now in darkness. J. a humped shape under the covers. Climbing in clumsily and noisily behind him. 'Please, J.' Vicious shrug-off of my arm. 'Leave me *alone.*'

Sitting in front of the toilet, fingers down my throat. Painful heaving followed by very painful retching followed by a small thin stream of puke.

Shivering now, climbing into bed, lying on my back, a taste of sick in my mouth.

'You're disgusting,' says J.

At the BBC I became a 'runner.' Running from the production office down to the studio. Calls for tea, sambos, combs, came through thick and fast. Where's 'Irish'? shouted the men. I need a coffee? Mineral water. A hair dryer.

I was the teenage hit in a wide-brimmed felt purple Biba hat and my mini skirt.

One of the MP's being interviewed offered a trip to the House of Commons? Sure, I said, lovely.

A brief tour, a rush, rush, drink in the MPs' bar, other MPs looking out knowingly from behind newspapers, then up to his panelled rooms. I'm pushed up against the door. He starts grabbing.

At first I thought it was a joke. He wasn't going to rape me in his rooms in the House of Commons, was he? Panting hard, his hand up my skirt trying to force down my tights, his eyes closed, his face closed and brick red.

I managed to yank the door open.

'You don't play by the rules!' he shouted after me down the corridor.

J. couldn't stop laughing. 'The jammy bastard' he said, opening a bottle of wine, 'The cheeky sod' he said, pouring generous glasses, much amused. Hahaha. We clinked glasses. When J. was happy, I was happy.

Inside though, I felt lost. Running from drink to food to sex. I made myself come in the bathroom. Frantic: 'Come you little bitch. *Come.*' Shopped compulsively. Hot and sweaty, I bought things that I hated as soon as I got them home.

'I don't *want* to go out,' J. said, 'You bore me.'

5

London Sister announced she was going to visit home. She wanted to show off her new baby. Dad, surprised and confused to hear that not only was she no longer trying to knock down the doors of the Vatican to get her man's marriage annulled, but she had made a baby, and wanted to bring it over to show him, began: No Daughter of Mine, She Shall Not Darken My Door! etc. etc. Mum put her foot down: Don't be ridiculous. OF COURSE we are going to welcome our first grandchild into the house.

In London I'd decided two things: one was to leave the man with his face turned to the wall. The other was to write to Dad and tell him that I had broken my promise to him. That I had in fact been living with the terrible man I'd sworn not to for the past four months. Ever since I moved to London.

Sorry, Dad. So, so, so sorry. Please please please forgive me?

I sat up at the grand piano in the ticking silence of the big empty drawing room, huge uncurtained Georgian windows glistening with navy night, writing my letter to Dad on blue notepaper, sipping whiskey.

It was after 1 am when I propped the finished letter on the music stand and went upstairs to bed.

The phone rang just after seven next morning. I ran down through the dark house. It was new Brother-in-Law. 'Your father died this morning.' The terrible hammer blow of shock, followed by a wailing sound—could it be me?—as I ran back up the stairs.

'Oh fuck,' said J., sitting up in bed.

Back at home Mum opened the front door, her eyes wet. 'Hello, Pet.' Death had smashed off her concrete carapace. She looked terrifyingly vulnerable. *'Mum.'*

Death had also smashed off the front of the house. And the back. Twin Sister, who had found Dad, kept saying, 'He was still warm, he was still warm,' to anyone who would listen. But we couldn't listen, each of us shattered inside our own whistling void. Everyone except the baby, who gurgled and fed and did little sick ups on London Sister's napkin'd shoulder. We patted the baby's warm bum. As if at any minute all of us, everyone and everything, might be lifted up and carried off into the void with Dad.

Dad, seized in death's terrifying clutches, lay on his back in a single bed at the top of the house. An Auschwitz skeleton. Yellow skin drawn tight over cheekbones.

All day, visitors called. Dad's brothers. Dad's sisters. Dad's priest brother. The men got whiskey. The wives, 'the aunts,' took tea with Mum. In the dining room. Dad's eldest brother—same cheekbones, same blue eyes, but everything sharper, harder—took my elbow:

42

'You seem very upset.' Upset? I wanted to smash the world to smithereens.

In the back garden the trees and bushes moved their leaves in a breeze as if nothing had happened. As if they had more right to life than Dad. In Dad's bedroom his leather shoes sat side by side under his chair. Shoes he'd worn the day before.

Dad.

Mum, sitting up in bed, eyes painted bright with grief, said to my sister: 'I never even said goodbye.'

O Mum.

Afterwards she went into hyperdrive—had the house painted, ordered new curtains for the drawing room. The older ones talked behind her back: she's being 'reckless.' I thought, better than sitting frozen. And anyway, it's her money; why shouldn't she spend it?

Before everyone left to go back to their lives Mum booked a photographer. Black and white prints show white faces, stretched stiff smiles. A family caught in the magnesium glare of death.

Gradually Mum reverted to frozen. Learned the bitter realities of widowhood in a patriarchal world—the phone not ringing, the post not bringing invitations to dinner or drinks. There was a terror in seeing her shriven, lined face at the hall door. The fireplace with two sods of smouldering turf. The empty fridge. Loneliness creeping like mould over everything. The more awful it was, the less any of us visited.

Twin Sister gave a supper party in her house. Mum got tipsy and went into the bedroom to 'have a little lie down.' I followed her in, pretty tipsy myself, swaying through the dark. Mum was lying on top of Twin Sister's bed, her shoes still on. 'Are you okay, Mum?'

Her eyes glittered in the half dark.

'You all loved your father more than me. You would all have

preferred him to live and me to die.'

I swayed over to the bed, grasping her icy hand.

'No, Mum! No *way!*'

But she was right. Not one of us ever stood by her. We were Daddy's girls.

Twin Sister, herself a little tipsy, said the night before Dad died London Sister had gone up to talk with him. Was up there, talking with him for hours.

'Did she tell him about me and J?'

Twin Sister looked across.

'You weren't exactly discreet.'

'She told Dad about me living with J?'

'She talked to him about lots of things.'

The first thing I saw when I got back to London was my 'letter of confession' still propped on the piano's music stand.

6

Kneeling over the lavatory, a long yellow streak of bile slid down the cracked bowl. 'I feel sick.' J. sat up. 'Jesus, you're pregnant' 'What?' 'We'll have to get a doctor' 'Why?' 'For an *abortion.*'

'Come on,' J. said, ' chop, chop.'

I was sent off to our black friend, Lionel, then to the restaurant and Tom, to ask for money.

Why couldn't J? I mean why couldn't he get the money from his bank? Why couldn't we do it ourselves? *No!* Did I not see how *dodgy* it would be if he paid out to an abortion clinic—from his personal account? How it would *look*? No, this was the only way.

'Anyway, don't worry,' he said as I was leaving for the clinic, his 'missus' had had three abortions. 'In in the morning, out in the afternoon.' He snapped his fingers. ' Just like that. Didn't knock a feather out of her.'

Next, a perfect Georgian square. A posh secretary with plunging décolletage and blood-red nails counted out my used notes. 'Mr. Simpson will see you now.'

Mr. Simpson held my completed form between finger and thumb as if it was contaminated. Looking over half-moon gold spectacles he asked, 'W4 or W1?'

I flushed. Instantly exposed as just another ignorant Irish girl looking for an abortion who didn't know the proper postcode for the false address she was giving.

'W1?' I stuttered.

Mr. Simpson pursed his lips. 'Quite.'

'I'll see you in the morning.'

'Tomorrow?'

'You do want this?' Again that contemptuous look over the half-rimmed gold spectacles.

The psychiatrist, two squares down, sat behind a desk in a living room crammed with cats, spider plants, magazines, books.

'You are definitely suicidal?'

I was busy extracting purrings from one of the cats. 'Sorry?'

'You'll be in danger of committing suicide if I don't sign this form?' he prompted.

The penny dropped.

'Oh. *Yes.*'

In the clinic it was: everyone knows what you're in here for so let's just get on with it.

'Just the date of your last period. Thank you.'

In the bed opposite, a woman sat up in a pink bed jacket. Knitting. *Jesus,* I thought, wait till I tell J! This middle-aged, middle class woman, prim as you please, *knitting,* while she waits to be wheeled in for an abortion. Can you beat that? Hahaha.

Wheeled in, legs unceremoniously grasped, strapped into steel stirrups, between their upturned vee as the doctor arrived through swing doors, masked, gloved hands aloft and the anaesthetist counted me down: twenny-three, twenny-two, twenny—

I came to in an upstairs room. Large uncurtained windows, a plane flying in a slowly descending arc right to left, its tail lights winking. J. appeared. He didn't have much time. He'd arranged to meet one of the ex-girlfriends he'd got the abortion doc's number from for a drink. Did I need anything? My insides felt as if I'd had twenty periods in a row. 'Something for the pain?' He'd ask on his way down.

Half an hour later one disprin arrived in a kidney dish.

I had a little cry.

7

Two days after the abortion J. announced that he'd booked us into a hotel in the country. 'In the Cotswolds,' he said, in a voice that implied I should be awed. And grateful. I would have preferred bed. Cups of tea, a glossy mag: Are you okay? Is there anything else I can get you? Are you sure now, darling girl?

Instead, it was up, throw some things into a bag and join him in the hire car he had parked out the front.

I didn't want to be in a strange car that smelt of Magic Tree air freshener, going off to a 'hotel in the Cotswolds.' I was 19, what did I care about the bloody Cotswolds? What did he care about them, come to think of it, Mr. So-Called Working Class, Angry Man Socialist?

I was still sore as well.

'Ready?' J. said, gunning the engine.

We drove out through the brutalist road system that surrounds London like a giant concrete spider's web. Cars. White vans. Thundering lorries. A pitiless traffic river.

'It's so *ugly*,' I said.

'What is?' J. snapped, glasses on, eyes on the road.

'All of it,' I said, gesturing at cement flyovers, four lanes of metal boxes hammering along.

'And how would you propose exiting the city?' J. asked in a voice that meant: you really don't have a clue about anything do you?

I started fiddling with the car radio: 'Carol King!'

'Not her again.'

It was dark before we reached our destination. And raining. J. was trying to remember the instructions he'd been given: first left out of the village, 500 yards down that road, at the first turn off, take the right fork—

'How do you know when it's 500 yards?' I asked.

'Oh for fuck sake,' he said, banging his hand down on the piece of paper in my lap, 'just read me the bloody instructions.'

Then there it was: a creeper covered, traditional stone Cotswold house converted into a small hotel. Warm yellow lights showed leaf-fringed windows, a man at a front porch unfolding an umbrella.

Shouldering his weekend bag, slamming his door to behind him, Mr. Angry Man Socialist transformed into Mr. Suave Man of the World hurried towards the figure in the doorway, hand outstretched: 'Bloody awful weather!'

'Awful!' echoed the figure in the doorway, eyeing me coming up behind in my miniskirt, my purple floppy hat from Biba, my laced, knee-high boots.

'I'll take you up to your room,' said our host, ignoring me.

The bedroom was two tightly sheathed divans, pleated, densely patterned florals, frilled skirts falling to the ground. The same pattern repeated on thickly pelmeted curtains, a low armchair, a Victorian glass-topped dressing table.

'Perfect,' said Mr. Angry Socialist.

The host, standing in the doorway, smiled, 'I'll see you downstairs.'

'Wonderful.'

The door clicked quietly to.

I climbed over the right hand divan to pull back the curtains and open a window. I stuck my face out into the night.

'What are you *doing*?'

'It's a bit claustrophobic here isn't it?' I said, raindrops like tiny needles on my skin.

J. lumped his weekend bag up onto the other bed.

'I'm going downstairs for a drink.'

Sitting on the toilet I felt something wet and warm slide out. I jumped up. The toilet bowl was bright red. 'I'm bleeding!' I shouted, lumps of bloody matter sliding down the sides of the bowl.

J. pulled open the bathroom door and began reefing sheets of toilet paper out from a metal dispenser. 'Here,' he said, 'shove these up you. You'll be fine.'

The toilet paper, the old fashioned kind, stiff and shiny, hurt as I pushed it up.

'Put on an extra pair of knickers,' J. said.

Then, impatient, standing at the door: 'I'll see you downstairs.'

Hobbling into the bedroom I pulled out the package the abortion clinic had provided. A sanitary belt and three sanitary towels. Individually wrapped. It reminded me of boarding school. The horror of an entire day spent with one towel—all that the nuns would allow. The terror of leakage. The smell when you took it off at night. Frantically scrubbing at heavily stained knickers with hard soap and cold water in the tiny toilet sink. Hauling wet knickers back on before getting into bed so they'd be dry for the morning.

Downstairs, our host, behind a gleaming bar, was engaged in animated chat with Mr. Suave.

'And what would, um, the young lady like?' he asked as I appeared. 'Give her a brandy,' Mr. Suave said. Our host placed a brandy balloon on the polished bar, holding the base with splayed fingers as he carefully poured. 'You might as well make that a double,' said Mr. Suave, patting my knee.'She's had a long day.'

The brandy slid down like liquid fire. Mr. Suave's hand, still proprietorial on my knee. 'I told you she could handle it' he smiled. Our Host, twisting the squeaking corked top back into the bottle, looked over the top of his glasses. Hmmm.

We were given a table in the centre of the dining room. Our host was most apologetic. He would have loved to have given us somewhere more private, one of the window seats for instance, but this was the 'regulars' night. He couldn't *not* look after them! His 'bread and butter.' Hahaha.

The same claustrophobic décor—thick curtains, table cloths dropping to an oxblood red carpeted floor, knives, forks, glasses, table mats, napkins crowding the table. 'Will you be having white or red?' asked Mr. Host, handing over the leather-bound Wine List.

Mr. Sauve's mood had improved dramatically with the 'pre-prandial snifters,' and the prospect of food. *'She,'* he said pointing at me, 'should probably have red. She needs building up.'

I smiled. He *cared!*

He looked briefly down the list.

'We'll have a bottle of your Fleurie.'

49

'Perfect,' said our host.

Warmed with brandy, delicious wafts of cooking aromas coming from the kitchen, I realised I was starving.

Our host, the Wine List held to his chest, asked: 'So what can we tempt you with?'

'Roast beef and Yorkshire pudding,' said J. 'Oxtail soup to start.' He slapped the menu shut. He indicated me with a finger: 'Same for her.'

'Excellent choice, if I may say so,' said our host. 'My wife's roast beef is a speciality of the house.'

'Lovely.'

The two men smiled at each other.

I smiled at J. again, lifting my glass. 'Bottoms up so!'

'Yes, *please*,' he said.

'You look like Mr. Wolf,' I said, laughing.

'I *am* Mr. Wolf' J. said, finishing off his sherry.

The food was delicious. Home-made oxtail soup, home-made soda bread, farm butter. Mains delivered on a large white plate with slices of pink roast beef, buttery yellow Yorkshire pud carefully positioned, its toes in aromatic gravy, two rounded mounds of creamy mashed potatoe, sliced roast carrots and parsnips. Glasses of velvet dark wine.

Yes.

J. finished before I did.

Chair pushed back, glass in hand, he eyed me across the table, a sly smirk on his face as I lifted another laden forkful to my mouth: 'I see you haven't lost your appetite anyway.'

I stopped.

Finishing off his glass, J. reached across for the bottle as I pushed my plate away.

'Don't let me put you off your food!' he laughed.

I pressed a linen napkin to my mouth.

'You should see your face!' laughed J.

'More wine?' he said.

Back upstairs, J. got undressed, throwing his clothes down on the armchair, climbing into the bed on the left. 'Good night so.' Could we not at least push the two beds together? 'No thank you,' J. said as he turned over on his side, jerking sheets and blankets up and over with him.

By the time I turned out the bedside light he was asleep. I lay in the dark. Scared to move in case the bloody mess inside my knickers opened up again.

The silence of the country pressed in all around.

The next day J. was up early and it was drive, drive, drive: this historic village, such and such a 'wold,' this sheep farmers' historic market. Village after village. They all seemed identical, posh historic lookalikes, forever preserved. Even the climbing roses around the doorways looked fake.

Usually J. would have laughed when I said, 'Even the climbing roses look fake.' Not today. No. Refusing to stop at a pub offering 'Warm Food. Hot Conversation,' saying, 'Probably too fake for you right?'

Why was he so angry?

'Who said I was angry?' he said. 'Maybe I'm just bored.'

The rain never stopped. The wipers of the hire car going side to side across the windscreen, sweeping curtains of wet from left to right, right to left to....

By the time we got home, J. wasn't even pretending conversation. He dropped me, before driving off to return the car. 'Will we go to the Italian and get a bite to eat when you get back?' I asked through the passenger window. 'No,' J. said; he was going to go to bed when he got back. I had been about as much fun 'to take on a trip as a basket of wet laundry. Less in fact.'

He leaned over, and wound up the window.

In the hall a postcard and two letters lay on the mat.

The postcard was from Mum. One of those ones with blue skies, bright green grass, red-haired children, a donkey, all in technicolour oranges, blues, greens, reds. Totally unlike the actual grey, green mistiness. 'Greetings from Ireland!' splashed across the top right corner in yellow italics.

'We are in Kerry,' Mum wrote in her familiar rounded hand. 'All having a good time. Hope you are well. Love, Mummy xxx.'

Holidays, I thought. Mum. Dad. The battered cream Cortina. Suitcases tied to the roof rack with skipping ropes. At the beach the little ones, water wings on, running to the waves curling up the beach, sliding back, Dad calling, 'Feet in only until a grownup comes!' The little ones squealing as the sea swirled around their bare feet in cold pearly rushes.

Letting my bag down onto a chair, I went downstairs to the kitchen.

The big old house, empty for three days, felt cold, malign. A pervasive silence highlighted by loud ticks from the carriage clock on the mantelpiece over the Aga. I sat at the large scrubbed table, my coat still on. I knew J. would never talk about it again. As far as he was concerned that was it: abortion debt paid.

8

J. had been offered a job in the South Pacific. An absolute bloody *dream* of a job. Sobbing wet messes of teenage girlfriends were not part of the dream. Sobbing wet messes of teenage girlfriends had become a right pain in the arse. Crying about their bloody dead father. Crying about their bloody dead abortion. 'If you wanted it that badly you should have gone ahead and had it. *Christ.*'

He hurried around London buying lightweight tropical suits. T-shirts. Shirts. Sun hats. Leather sandals. Swimming trunks. Notebooks. A new washbag. New briefcase. Laying everything out on the double bed. Everything top quality. No expense spared.

PART THREE

'Promises are worse than lies. You don't just make them believe, you also make them hope.'

Marilyn Monroe

1

The pay phone at the end of the Pearl Bar bar rang. Working in the obituary section of The Irish Times, I was having Friday drinks. Maeve Binchy, Dick Walsh, Dick Grogan, Maeve Donellan, Nell McCafferty were all noisily gathered around two marble-top tables pushed together and covered with glasses, pints of Guinness, a hot whiskey, a half pint of lager, smeared empty glasses, ashtrays choking with butts, an abandoned cigarette still burning.

As soon as the phone rang I knew it was him. The barman held up the receiver, 'For you, Sweetman.'

'I'm in Australia!' J.'s faraway voice said down a whistling line. 'Oh' I said.

'*Oh!*' he shouted. 'Is that all you've got to say? I've wangled a trip back. 'When will I see you?'

Glancing back at the noisy group of writers and photographers, I turned, cupped my hand over the receiver, 'When are you coming?' Whistling and crackling on the line increased. I made out 'London' and 'Tuesday.'

'I can't hear,' I said.

'London!' J. shouted. 'I'll be there Tuesday. Ring you from there!'

'Lover boy?' Nell McCafferty asked as I sat back down.

I laughed, embarrassed, and leaned in to pick up my beer. How had she guessed?

'You'd better get rid of the other one so,' said Nell, picking up her glass.

J. stood at the door of my basement flat, black leather weekend bag over his shoulder, passport and ticket in hand, seasoned international traveller, grinning '*Hello!*' At the counter of my little kitchen, my back to him, I said, 'Would you like some coffee?' I heard the thump of his bag hitting the floor, then he was pressing himself in, his right hand reaching between my legs: 'I'd like to fuck you. Right here. Right now.' He swivelled me around to face him. '*Jesus!* I've missed this,' hands cupping my bottom: 'Don't tell me you haven't missed it too!'

On the third day, arm in arm, we met the other boyfriend on the street. 'Some feminist you are,' he said coldly.

J. asked, 'Who was that?' 'Oh just someone.'

On his last evening J. booked a table in The Shelbourne. His knee pushed between mine under the white tablecloth, he raised his glass 'Miss Blue Eyes,' wine the colour of nectar tipping sideways, 'I want you to come out and join me. I want us never to be apart ever again. I want you AT MY SIDE. Okay?'

Had I ever been happier?

Three days after his departure, two hot whiskies in, coins for the phone reluctantly prised from the barman, I rang London.

Twin Sister answered the phone. 'Hello, how ARE you?' Very jolly.

'I'm, I'm okay,' I said, taken aback. 'What are you doing there?'

Twin Sister laughed, 'I'm here to *help*.'

'Help with what?' She laughed again, 'They're painting their flat!' 'Uh, okay. Is J. there?'

'We're just about to put a leg of lamb in the oven! Will I get him to ring you back?'

I stood stuck to the ground, the receiver in my hand, staring at the heavy black and brass oblong of the payphone box riveted to its wooden frame against the wall, telephone numbers in biro driven into the soft wood, the mouthpiece sticky from previous, inebriated calls.

Fucking *fuck*, I thought, *she's SLEEPING with him. She's sleeping with him!*

Unused coins clattered down into the receptacle as I pressed Button B. I thought I might faint.

On the way home I bought a bottle of whiskey. Two packets of painkillers. Cold musty air exhaled out of the flat as I opened the door. Everything looked suddenly cheap, hideous. In the mottled mirror over the basin a frightened white face looked back.

I sat in the middle of the unmade bed, in the damp basement room, tearing open the painkillers. A handful of white tablets in one hand, whiskey bottle in the other, I swallowed, gagging as the hard white tablets stuck in my throat.

Same again.

I must have passed out.

I woke in darkness. A feeling of crawling dread. The wall to the left of the bed began bulging inwards. Twin sister emerged into the room. Smiling. 'You're *sleeping* with him!' I said. Twin Sister smiled more.

I passed out again.

In the morning, I rang the office to say I had to go to the dentist. An emergency. I met Nell McCafferty. 'What's the matter with yew? You look shite.'

I didn't trust myself to get words out.

Four days later I came back to the flat to find Twin Sister standing in the sitting room. I could feel myself filling up, like a tyre over inflating: '*Did* you sleep with him?' Twin Sister half turned: 'He's very fond of you, you know.'

I walked out to the kitchen, blood stampeding through my veins. The little kitten from upstairs was at the window, black tail upright, vibrating, tiny pink mouth opened in a mew. Shaking, I splashed milk into a chipped saucer, put it at the back door. Lap, lap, lap, spots of milk sticking to the tiny whiskers.

I stood at the opened door staring at the yard with its bulging bins, broken mop, wet coir mat unravelling on the moulded concrete step, the metal flaps of an extractor on the outside toilet flapping like a faulty valve, the tall Georgian houses, side walls roughly cemented, reached up and up, trapping a dull grey sky between them, hefty clouds barely moving, a single mewling seagull, the same dull grey as the clouds, wheeling.

2

When J. got back three months later I asked him. He laughed: 'You could hardly expect me to turn down an opportunity like that now could you?'

'But *did* you?'

We were in the car. He poked my thigh, laughing. 'You're not jealous of your own *sister* are you?!'

I felt confused. 'No, it's just— '

'Just what?' he said, poking harder.

'I—' I began.

'Ridiculous!' J. said, poking harder, 'You're *ridiculous!*'

He had to concentrate then, we were coming into traffic.

3

J. wanted me to come to Africa with him.

I had a commission to write my first book, a non-fiction look at Ireland of the 70s, *On Our Knees*. 'The great are only great because we are on our knees, Let us arise!' I had found an agent in London, Nicholas Thompson, thanks to journalist Maureen Cleave. He gave dinner parties to introduce me to his other authors—James Cameron, Madhur Jaffrey, famous grown-ups being very sweet to a gash 22-year-old, Ms. Wild 'Arrish.

I was going to be published!

I moved home and back in with Mum. I had a little green manual Olivetti, a present from J. A clunky tape recorder, often discarded as tapes got chewed up, ran out, or the batteries expired. Sometimes listening was better—you had to concentrate harder knowing there was no back-up. I had shorthand notebooks. Biros. A list of profiles that developed from interview to interview: 'Oh you should talk to so and so.' I travelled by bus, train, hitchhiker's thumb.

At home I thundered away all day in the basement. In the evening Mum and I ate supper together, then she went back upstairs to read that day's pages. The publisher had the typed manuscript in just under nine months.

Among my interviewees were Cathal Goulding, Sean Mac Siotfain, Charlie Haughey, Desmond Guinness, John McKeague, Mary Anderson, Dan McCarthy.

On Our Knees hit the bestseller list, sold 60,000 copies within weeks and caused a stir. Who was this young one giving out about Charlie Haughey, Far Right Catholicism and the Provisional IRA?

Nell McCafferty rang: 'Well aren't you the cheeky young one?'

Then I was in the skies and off to join J. in Africa. I dedicated *On Our Knees* to him: 'To J., with whom this book wouldn't have been possible.' He looked hurt. 'But it's *true*,' I laughed, 'when I'm with you I can never do anything.'

Oh, *Africa*.

First the heat. The door of the plane opens, a blast of oven-hot air, a furnace into which you have to step, sweat already running down your armpits as you cross the tarmac, in a full-length cotton dress that a friend had pulled over her head at the goodbye party the night before, 'Take this! Think of me!' Shivering in it at Heathrow, under the African sun it felt like burlap sacks.

J. had been assigned a UNDP (United Nations Development Programme) bungalow. A white shoe box with identical white shoe boxes scattered on an unlandscaped shale clearing. Inside a Scandinavian-style sparse living room, small kitchen, small bathroom, bedroom. At ceiling height, very small oblong windows covered in wire mesh netting, a small veranda from which you could see the other, identical chalets.

Apart from the heat, we could have been in an upmarket housing development in Dublin.

Oh.

When J. had gone to work I took a chair and my coffee and sat out. Agnes, the maid, followed, agitated. 'Nobody sit out like this, Memsahib.' Hand over her eyes, she glanced up at the sun dangling, burning, in the sky above us, carried my coffee back inside, shaking her head.

At the weekend J. got me a petrol scooter. I rode to the shops, the tyres sinking into boiling silky sand. On the way back a lizard, the size of a large dog, shouldered his way up out of the scrub onto the roadway. I fell off the bike. He stared out from his ancient dinosaur eyes, lid flipping front to back, then slowly jack-knifed his body back down and into the bush.

I was still shaking when I got back. 'But it was HUGE.' J. couldn't stop laughing.

A German hydrologist living next door pushed a note under the door: 'Next two week I am gone to home. Please to suicide Nuala when I am leaving.' We laughed behind our door at his terrible English. And his terrible attitude. Suicide his beautiful Siamese cat? At that moment purring, her chocolate brown velvet tail wrapped around my bare legs. No way!

J. was working as an Economic Consultant, an Agricultural

Advisor. He wrote reports. Hundreds of pages of detailed information: what giving a tractor to a village will cost over ten years, the amount of acreage it will plough, the amount of spares that will be needed, the amount of seed, fertiliser needed. Spreadsheet after spreadsheet. One night an English friend came over with his wife. Working class, from Birmingham. 'It's all bollix really, isn't it?' he said. 'The farmers out here know more about farming than a hundred of us expat "experts" together.' The two men laughed, clinked beers.

Was it all bollix?

J. and I made friends with the Socialists working at the University. Walter Rodney was visiting, 'How Europe Underdeveloped Africa.' We met the President, Julius Nyrere, 'Mwalimu' at a reception. Slender. Graceful. An ex-freedom fighter desperate to lift his people out of poverty. Out of the destruction that colonialism leaves behind.

Dar Es Salaam, 'the haven of peace,' was a handful of modernist skyscrapers, hotels and office blocks, then low squat buildings, once creamy stucco, now peeling, with thick walls, deep balconies, crumbling beauties left behind by the Germans and British. Mile upon mile of shanty towns.

Rich whites lived in the best parts of town, behind high walls and massive, locked gates. The Asian community, shipped in as 'indentured' labour by the Brits during colonial times to build the railways, came next. Then Tanzanian professionals and civil servants. Finally, the vast majority in the shanty towns—concrete shacks, crammed together either side of open drains.

I got a job on *The Daily News,* the English language daily for expats and civil servants, sharing a desk with legendary Features Editor, Philip Ocheing.

One day I took photos down at the fish market. Black and white film, developed myself in the darkroom. Young women, running from the camera, covered their faces with their burkas, laughing. The black of their burkas in brilliant contrast to the midday sun's glare, the snow-white fish. I couldn't wait to show them off. Philip was outraged. How dare I come to Africa and take photos of his Muslim sisters who clearly didn't want to be photographed, who were actually RUNNING AWAY from my nasty little white girl camera. *What was I bloody thinking?* Standing, hot in the face, the newsroom gone deathly silent, I wanted to crawl into a hole.

J. got up at 7am and headed off in short sleeved shirt, lightweight pants, black sandals. I didn't have to be in till ten. I decided to try and write a novel. To see if I could. I sat in my bikini at a desk in our bedroom, at my little green Olivetti, while Agnes mopped the floors and did the washing up. The postman, in enormous colonial khaki shorts and white pith helmet, arrived on his black bike. Agnes made coffee. The outside world heated up and up, and here I was at my desk writing about Ireland. Grey skies. Damp days. Boarding school. Parlours. The coldness of the nuns. The coldness of everything.

When I'd finished I parcelled the manuscript up in brown paper and string, biked down to the General Post Office and sent it off to Nicholas in London. Five weeks later a letter arrived—Michael Joseph want to publish!

That evening J. and I had arranged to meet friends in a bar near the beach. Delicious cold beer. Tapas of hot sliced potatoes, olives, sardines, in dark green saucers. Two beers in, I tell them about my novel. The letter from the publishers.

J. astonished, slid his arm around me, ordered more beers: 'And you did it all without telling anyone!'

Our friends raised their glasses, 'Bloody hell!'

'To Ireland's next great novelist!' said J.

I was warm with happiness. Basking in the glow of J's admiration.

J. said it was about time I got an IUD fitted. 'We don't want you getting bloody pregnant again.' At the hospital, after the fitting, the doctor said to J., 'Your wife has a very low pain threshold.' I pretend-laughed.

That night J. developed a fever. He said he felt as if he had a Kilner jar rolling around inside his head. I lay on the other bed, bent double, Ah, ah, ah, ah. J. said I'd have to get up and phone the doctor. He thought he might have malaria. His temperature was 104. His head exploding. I dragged myself to the phone. The doctor, a heavy drinker, was already pissed. I described J.'s symptoms. 'Very likely malaria. Put him in a bucket of cold water. Okay?' I explained I wasn't talking about a dog, we didn't have a dog. I was talking about J.

I went to the doctor's house to collect painkillers and anti-malaria meds. The doc, very red in the face, pointed to the chicken wire cage in the corner where his two parrots lived. The bigger one, bony prehensile claws still hooked around his perch, was upside down. 'Said his last Fuck Off!' the doctor laughed, tears bright in his eyes as he handed me a tumbler of local gin, Konyagi, 'Bottoms up!'

J. and I lay inside our mosquito net in the dark listening to the mosquitos' sewing machine whine as they circled. He laughed when I told him about the doctor. And the dead parrot. 'Don't make me laugh! It hurts!'

One night J. went, *Ssshh*. He pointed to a corner of the room. A knife was very carefully slicing down through the wire mosquito netting. A long pole then pushed in through the hole, a rough home-made hook swinging at the end. 'Someone's fishing,' J. whispered. The hook hovered over our new iron, then lifted it slowly and carefully towards the window. 'We should go after them!' 'Are you mad?' said J. 'Do you want to get killed over an iron?' J. said it was time to show me some of the 'real' Africa. He bought a tent and a Campingaz stove and we set off for Ngorongoro. Home to the Maasai. *Ngoro. Ngoro.*

Inside the park we were alone. No wardens. No fences. No signs. No houses. Alone in the Garden of Eden. Herds of giraffe and zebra cantered by, acacia trees dotted across the grasslands, low, smoky blue mountains in the distance. First hyenas. Like hysterical shoppers in old fur coats, snarling, squealing, biting, a ragged circle around a half-eaten carcass. 'Impala,' J. said, 'poor bastard.' The impala, its beautiful head still intact, beautiful eye staring out, is thumped this way and that as the hyenas scream and swarm. Vultures sit in the thorn bushes nearby, cruelly hooked orange beaks, hideous scrawny necks, ragged brown feathers and orange legs, waiting their turn.

'Let's go,' I urged, 'they're vile.' The smell of blood, piss, hot stinking fur overwhelming. 'This place would be fucked without them,' J. said.

Zebra next. Plump roundy bottomed cartoons with their carefully painted on stripes, tails vigorously switching flies. A giraffe, head poking up through a tree, huge quizzical eyes, stared down. By the water hole the hippos soaked in the cappuccino-coloured river, glistening bulge of eyes and nostrils just above the water.

We stopped. Took out the cold box. Poured coffee from J.'s flask. I took out my cigarettes. Blue smoke drifted up into the dome of blue overhead.

Two young Maasai appeared. Lean, ebony black. Piercing black eyes surveying us. Festooned with tightly beaded earrings and neck pieces, wrapped in their trademark bright red cloth, they were sensationally beautiful. Would they like a coffee? A cigarette? They would indeed. *'Ndio.'* I tried not to stare. They studied us openly and keenly, smiled at my pidgin Swahili. What do we look like to them, I wondered when they'd gone. Slow, overweight clueless strangers in their land? 'Speak for yourself,' J. said, throwing the last of the coffee on the ground.

J. insisted we camp out. Get the full safari experience. He'd brought wine, steaks, bread. Our blue tent seemed tiny in the huge dark, teeming now with layer upon layer of sound. Countless thousands of crickets, croaking frogs, a trampling, a whistle answered by another whistle. A deafening cacophony.

J. woke me in the 'small' hours, a hand over my mouth. 'There's an elephant outside. Don't make a sound.' Still half asleep he man-handled me into the car's opened maw. Crawling in himself, he pulled the hatchback door carefully down. Through the windows, rimed with dust, we watched the huge body, the trunk sweeping side to side over the campground, swishing along the side of the tent. Africa suddenly so close. One shove from that huge body and we were meat inside a tin can.

In the morning we found elephant droppings. Brown footballs. A warning? Stay the fuck out of my Garden of Eden?

The second night we stayed in a rondavel owned by a private safari company. Dinner was served on a platform looking out over the dark vastness. During the second course the waiter hurried to our table: 'A lion has been heard, Bwana. Close, close.' We heard a long, low growl in the hot dark. Diners rushed to the railing.

The days got hotter and hotter. More and more humid. Everyone tired. Everyone longing for the monsoon to arrive. A friend from the UK came to stay. Night fell, then a thundering; the raindrops the length of knitting needles smashed onto the patio announcing the monsoon's arrival. We ran outside laughing, shouting under the hot deluge.

It rained and rained and rained and rained. The drains on the roadside, swollen with rushing ochre-coloured floods as mould bloomed on everything. Our leather sandals. Leather suitcases. The lens of my camera. Agnes brought bleach. Soon the whole chalet smelled like an undertakers. 'No bleach,' I said. Agnes could not understand. 'Bleach good, Memsahib.' I held my nose. 'Bleach bad.' Agnes thought I was crazy.

At night J. listened to the BBC World Service. News of bombs going off in Belfast. Bernadette Devlin, tiny, brilliant and furious. Blurry photographs in the *International Herald Tribune* of young guys, scarves over their mouths hurling bricks, petrol bombs. Armed British soldiers walking back to back down the Falls Road, women with headscarves over their hair curlers, arms crossed, watching from their doorways. The 'Reverend' Ian Paisley bawling out his bile. 'Tough bastard,' J. said.

I was filled with a sudden, sickening longing for grey skies. Wet pavements. Grafton Street. Stephen's Green. Anything green. Our kitchen. *Home.*

Expat lives revolved around embassy parties. The British Embassy. The German Embassy. The Cuban Embassy. Cuba giving the best parties. Whole roast hog. Cold boxes stacked with beers. Music. Laughter. Much slagging off of *gringos.*

J. and I specialised in getting pissed, teaming up with anyone who looked game—outsiders, writers, socialists, oddballs. J. delighted to have me at his side, his revolutionary *Oirish* feminist, his young one. Who loved to drink. Argue. Jump fully clothed into embassy pools. Get others to jump in too. Ignoring the annoyed looking face of the Ambassador's wife. Laughing at their *We are not amused,* expressions.

We *are* amused! More cocktails please!

4

Then I had a fling. I didn't intend to, but he was tall, rangy, bearded, sandalled. A NICE guy who ran one of the NGOs. Sweet, gentle, funny. We got tipsy together at an embassy 'do.' What could J. say? He was forever boasting about all the fucks he'd had in Africa. The multitudinous extra marital couplings he and his friend Mike had had. Hahaha.

Sauce for the goose was sauce for the gander, right? Hadn't we liberated 70s kids done away with all that exclusivity nonsense?

Sure we had.

J. had gone 'up country' on a work safari. By chance, the nice man's wife and their three sons were also up country. The Nice Guy and I, very tipsy, got to their house and ended up in bed.

Their house—a real *rondavel,* with thatched palm roof, deep balcony running right around, insides crammed with local furniture, African ebony sculptures, Tinga Tinga paintings, bright kangas—was everything I'd thought J.'s and my place would be.

A lovely weekend. Eating. Swimming. Visiting Tanzanian bars where he spoke fluent Swahili. Knew what to order.

J. arrived back a day early.

He walked into our kitchen just as Nice Guy was taking ice out of the fridge and immediately smelt a rat. 'Time for you to go,' he said. Nice Guy left without a word, head lowered. I thought of two male dogs. Walking around each other carefully, on stiff legs, ruffs bristling.

J. threw his things on the bed. Said we were going out for dinner. *Now.* After a couple of glasses of wine he asked me what was going on. I did a garbled, oh so jolly, explain: sauce for the goose is sauce for the gander! A little *flirtation* being good for the soul! It was *nothing!*

Jollity died in my throat when I met J's eyes. That night's love making felt more like punishment than love.

J. decided we should get married. 'Putting your brand on me!' I laughed. But he didn't laugh. 'It makes sense, from a tax point of view,' he said, snapping shut the clasps on his briefcase.

J. asked Nice Guy, whose wife was still away, to be our witness. I hadn't had the courage to tell him what had really happened, so off we three set at 8 in the morning, the air already packed with heat, Nice Guy carrying a Tinga Tinga painting, a wedding present from him and his wife.

Fuck.

At the registry office, the clerk asked J., 'Which kind of marriage you wish to have Bwana? Monogamous, Polygamous or Potentially Polygamous?' J. laughing loudly, said, 'Potentially Polygamous of course!'

At the supermarket the men bought a crate of beer and we went to the beach to sit on a narrow shelf of hot yellow sand, tall curving coconut trees, topknots crackling in the breeze, behind us. Perched on scorching shale tilting down to the Indian Ocean, a cerulean blue, we watched as the waves thumped and sucked back with a fierce undertow. Arab dhows, black against the intense blue, wooden rigging creaking as they inched across the horizon. Young boys, machete in one hand, green coconut in the other, offered: 'Coconut, Memsahib?' An expert decapitation, then the green fruit, brimming with fragrant juices, was handed over.

70

Finally, Nice Guy said he had to go. 'Some work to do.'

Goodbyes against a blaring sun. J. and I packed up the empties and headed home.

The Wedding Day was over.

5

An unexpected knock on the door on a Saturday afternoon a week later. It was Nice Guy's wife. 'I need to talk to *her*,' she said, pushing past J. and into the living room. On the sofa, she signalled for me to sit beside her. She looked up briefly at J., still wondering what was going on, and said: 'I need to talk to her, *alone.*'

Quaking, I sat down.

Very calm, very controlled, very *very* furious, Nice Guy's wife said her husband had told her everything. She would therefore be grateful if I didn't lie. She held up a hand to indicate how certain she was; she did NOT want to be bullshitted.

Eh, okay.

She was here to extract a promise: I was never *ever* to come near her husband, or her family, or her house, ever again. 'Is That Quite Clear?'

Um, *yes?* I mumbled.

Would I please make that promise to her? Here. Now? She sat, very upright, very certain, mouth pinched.

'I...I promise.'

I heard something drop behind the living room door. J. was *listening.*

As soon as she was gone the door burst open and J. rushed in. He chased me into the bathroom. The bedside lamp came crashing down on my head, shade and bulb shattering, as J., his face distorted, screamed: 'You bitch, you fucking, fucking little *bitch.'*

Bash, smash, crash.

I ran out past him to the living room, grabbed his shortwave radio, and smashed it on the tiled floor, the plummy BBC world service voice still going as he snatched it up and smashed it again against the wooden arm of the sofa.

We smashed plates, ashtrays, tore down the shower curtain (a satisfactory clattering of metal rings onto the tiled floor), the generic photo of Africa on the living room wall, more plates.

By evening, and the early tropic dark, we were spun out. Love making was followed by food, was followed by more lovemaking, was followed by whiskey.

Lying on our backs in the dark, J. started talking about his childhood.

I could not keep my eyes open. J. kept prodding me awake: 'I'm telling you the most important things in my life and you're falling asleep.'

It was true. I had begged and pleaded with him to tell me about his past. What had happened that was so terrible? Why had he run away from home at 16? Why had he never gone back? Why had he never *ever* been in touch with his parents, his brother, anyone from his home village? *Ever?* Not even a letter or a phonecall? *Why?*

What had happened?

Now here he was talking about it all: his mother's adoration of him following the stillbirth of her first son. His father's jealousy. His childhood dysfunction, crapping his pants up to the age of seven. His father's farm labourer's fury, home from work, roaring into the little thatched cottage, smelling shit, seeing Mum washing the little boy in the steel bath in front of the stove, Dad grabbing him naked and wet out of the bath, his Mum's screams, his little boy screams, as Dad, wielding a thatching pole the size of a rolling pin, beat the little wet body again, again. And again.

Good *god*.

No wonder you ran away. No wonder you couldn't fucking wait to get out of the place. No wonder you ran and didn't stop till you got to Canada. Got a job on the railways by pretending to be 18. Got raped by the hard chaws. Nothing to be done. No one to turn to. No one to tell.

OhmyGod you poor thing

After eighteen months on the railways J. hitched his way back to the UK, to London. He knew a dead end when he saw one. But in all that time he never wrote home. Never phoned home. Not even to let them know he was alive.

No.

Then he was in London aged 19, studying at the London School of Economics. Met his wife. For the first two years of their relationship he pretended to be Canadian. It was only when their baby boy arrived, and she wanted to show him off to the grandparents, that J. was forced to come clean. How did that go down? J. the slick cosmopolitan Canadian turned out to be working class J. from a labourer's thatched cottage in Lincolnshire. She was a bit shocked alright. But he got around her.

'Are you awake?' J. prodded again. 'Are you listening to me?' 'Mmm, mmm.' Every cell in my body screamed out for sleep.

I tried to get J. talking again the next day. But the steel gates had ground shut again. No, he did not want to talk about it. It was over. Right?

'But you were abused!'

'No I fucking wasn't.'

'You *were*. You were beaten on your little wet seven year old body with a thatching pole. Couldn't we take the day off? Go to the beach. *Talk?*'

'If you don't stop I'll never talk about any of it ever again.'

'You won't talk about it even though what happened to you very likely destroyed your first marriage? Led to you abusing your son?'

'Fuck off. Go away. I'm getting ready for work.'

'Even though it could be destroying ours?'

'Fuck *off.*'

A few days later J. exacted his revenge.

I came home at midday to find him padding around in his bathing trunks, looking for one of my bikinis. He was off to the beach! In the middle of a working day? *Yes!* There was this journalist visiting from *The Guardian.* I *know!* He was taking her to the beach for the afternoon! Now, where did I keep my bikinis? She needed to borrow one.

Of course she was blonde, beautiful, slim, intelligent, witty, sophisticated, *ironic.* 'Sauce for the goose, sauce for the gander!' J. laughed as he hurried out.

It went on for days until, weeping, I went to friends, filmmakers Gary and Paula Belkin. They listened, gave me an omelette and a cold beer, then Gary said, Come on. He was going to drive me home.

J. and the *Guardian* journalist were sitting side by side on our sofa. 'Up you get,' Gary said to Ms. Ironic. 'I'll drive you into town.' Cool as fuck up she got and walked out into the dark. J. stayed sitting. Gary said, 'I've no idea what's going on but you'd better sort it out.' J. nodded. Gary left.

I found my bikini, my favourite, hooked over the balcony rail. Next day, down at the beach I pushed it in among a pile of discarded coconut shells. Their bearded hoary husks flamed up, blue smoke trembling in the scorching overheated air.

Overnight I developed diarrhoea. Everytime I ate something there would be a gurgling, followed by a panicked rush to the loo. Everyone was convinced I had amoebic dysentery. Weight fell off. I could feel it falling off, like melting snow sliding off a roof. I felt light headed. Other worldly.

Paula looked worried. Gary looked worried. With their help I got a flight back to London and London Sister. The doctor at the Ministry of Overseas Development was excited. 'Amoebic dysentery, well, well.' But I didn't think I had amoebic dysentery. I think I wanted to disappear.

'He was just boasting, darling,' London Sister's friend said, looking into her glass, making the ice bump side to side, as she fingered out the lemon slice. 'You *never* take them at their word. And you never *EVER* tell them about your affairs. Particularly not a guy like him.'

I wanted to ask her what 'a guy like him' was like. I wanted to ask her how she knew. How did one find out what they did, or didn't, like? The doorbell rang. It was J. He'd walked off the UNDP job in Dar and followed me to London.

What?

Another friend of London Sister and her gin-drinking friend came to the house. That night in bed I said to J., 'You slept with three of the women in that room tonight!' Delighted, J. said, 'Indeed and I did!'

Even as I said it I wondered why did I congratulate him on being a philandering Don Juan, when him being a philandering Don Juan was killing me?

6

My novel, *Fathers Come First*, was published.

The hardback edition with a gothic marvel of a cover—a plump crucified doll impaled on a crucifix with feminism's logo in place of INRI fixed to the cross—sold 2,000 copies in a couple of months. Pan Books scooped up the paperback rights and it sold another 60,000.

The senior editor at Pan took me out to lunch to celebrate. Back to his apartment after. That awful, stomach churning moment when you see the men going pink, breathing harder, eyes glazing over. I was to sit close. *Closer!* I thought you were a liberated woman! He pulled my wide-necked t-shirt top down, revealing naked shoulders, then no bra. Panting he whispered I should always wear my tops thusly. Did I know how beautiful I was?

I finally escaped. Confused and dishevelled, I hurried past the doorman downstairs. He looked up, shocked, as I fled.

The editor wasn't a bad man. Mauling young ones was what men got away with in those days. It didn't occur to me to complain. He was the boss.

Bunked down in London Sister and her husband's front room, a fan heater underneath the desk, I tried to work up a film script about a French woman who believed she was a witch, which agent Nicholas had wangled for me. J. sat at a desk beside me and worked on a report.

Like other friends home from Africa, crouched inside overheated rooms, too large dogs beside them, dull-haired and dull-eyed, Africa glowed ever brighter on the horizon, a longed for, impossibly out of reach, Shangri La.

J. said he couldn't *stand* England. The cold. The boredom. The fucking greyness.

Eventually the Ministry for Overseas Development, none too happy with him for walking off the job in Tanzania, offered new postings: The Philippines, Central America, Honduras, Peru, or the Amazon? Which did I fancy?

In a new country J.'s mood would improve dramatically. A new hotel. A new house. A new household to set up. New people. New work. New countryside to explore. Sunshine.

Inevitably the newness wore off and J.'s mood would start sagging again. I AM SO FUCKING BORED. Everyone, and everything, was boring. Only a new person, usually a woman, would wake him up. The lights would snap on. The engine would be gunned. He was off.

PART FOUR

'Home is not where you live, but where they understand you.'

Christian Morganstern

1

Travelling was amazing. Wherever J. was posted, I got work too. Writing. Journalism. Doing assessments for NGOs like Oxfam or Concern. Taking photos. My salary was never close to J.'s super duper 'foreign expert' take, deposited into a tax free account in the Channel Islands, living expenses, and housing, covered by the UN, or whoever the contracting agency was, but I always had a job. Some money of my own, and a way to better understand the country we were in.

J. said he didn't want a house of our own. He said it was cheaper to get the government 'to pay for one's housing.' Or stay with friends. It meant living in government housing when we were away, or staying with London Sister and her husband when we were in London, with Mum in Ireland. But I was 27. I really, *really* wanted a place of our own.

Eventually J. agreed. If I found a place, and arranged the fixing up, he'd pay.

We decided on Dublin. I found an artisan cottage ten minutes walk from the city centre and nabbed it for IR£6,000. The doing-up would be another IR£6,000 and we were good to go. Rugs and blankets from Mexico and Peru. Tinga tinga paintings and ebony sculptures from Tanzania. Pottery from the Amazon and Oaxaca. Stripped pine furniture from Twin Sister.

Home!

J. had a love-hate relationship with Ireland. He loved the artists, the poets, the writers who congregated around McDaids and The Bailey. The crazy drinking sessions. The music. He loved the countryside. Achill Island. Kerry. Connemara. But he raged against 'the fuckers' who wouldn't open the door, even a crack, to an out of work English development economist.

He wasn't very good at selling himself. One trip to chat with one economist about possibilities that produced nothing resulted in days of recriminations—'this stupid blindfolded fucking *backwater* of a country.' Followed by refusals to try again.

I was offered a diary column for the *Sunday Independent*. I loved it, cycling down to Middle Abbey Street with my copy every week. Then J. was offered short-term desk work at the Ministry of Overseas Development in London. Writing up reports. Staying at London Sister and her husband's house during the week, coming home to Dublin at weekends. We decided he should take it.

After a couple of months it wasn't 'worth' coming home every weekend. There wasn't time. He was writing fucking reports for chrissake, not on bloody holiday. How could I not see that?

I rang London Sister. What was going on? 'No smoke without fire,' was her cryptic reply. So he *was* having an affair with someone? I should ring J. I rang J. He said he didn't want to 'talk about it over the phone.' He would come home at the weekend.

I felt like a kid: pooh-poohed for being a scaredy cat only to open the door and find an axe murderer.

I SCREAMED down the phone at J. You fucking bastard, you PRICK, you liar, you BASTARD. The young French guy renting the spare room emerged, hands pressed to his ears. 'I 'ope I never 'ave to fight with *yoo*.'

I sat in the kitchen in bra and pants with the French guy, slaughtering a bottle of whiskey until tears came. Tears of rage. Then I phoned J. and told him to fuck off. To stay fucked off. Then fuck off some more. Then I had sex with the French guy. He was sweet and attentive and quirky. 'I can feel my sex getting 'arder,' he would say, hand over his private parts. My women friends all said he was GORGEOUS. Meaning: dump the English guy and set up with Mr. Sexy French Guy.

Fate had something else in store.

2

I met writer Aidan Higgins at a party in John and Nuala Mulcahy's beautiful drawing room in Ranelagh. He'd just been awarded a bursary. I had a commission for a new book and a place on Tony Cronin's writing course in Galway. Reeling from my broken marriage, I agreed to Aidan's plan: 'Let us go and live by the sea in Connemara and write books.'

I'm horribly ashamed to say I didn't consider how his wife, Jill, might feel. She and their three boys in their flat in Muswell Hill. I was suddenly, madly, in love with this witty, adorable, *clever* man.

We found a cottage on a tiny inlet alongside a pub by a pier draped in skirts of glistening umber seaweed rising and falling on incoming tides of purest lapis lazuli, the ridiculously beautiful, crumpled blue Paul Henry mountains all around.

In the evenings we cooked mussels. Spuds direct from the landlord's garden. Drank wine. Built up turf fires in the open grate. We swam naked in the lapis lazuli lakes. Drank pints in the pub owned by our landlord where gruff Connemara men, 'the Singing Stones,' who didn't utter all evening, suddenly broke into heart-breaking Sean Nós.

Two days a week we drove into Galway. The rust-covered car friends had given us braving the winter storms, waves lashing over the sea wall at Salthill, the road awash with swirling sudsy water, rocks, pebbles, Aidan shouting, 'Keep going! Keep going! Don't stop or we're banjaxed entirely!'

For Aidan, writing was *the* sacred art. Cliches were the Devil's spawn. Pathetic fallacies produced an allergic reaction. When I showed him pages of a novel I'd done, so heart-breaking I kept crying over it myself, he scrawled: 'Who are these dreadful people?'

'If only you would write like you *speak*,' he'd say as I whacked out yet another piece of cliché-clotted journalese.

One weekend in a cottage on a hillside in Mayo, my neighbour shouted across her fuchsia hedge, Would I not come in? She had a bottle of whiskey and two tumblers. When I was leaving two hours later she stood at her little gate: 'You should *shtay* with that man,' she indicated the cottage, and Aidan, 'He has more *nature* in him than that other lad.' A vast blue Mayo sky, white clouds racing each other, reeled overhead. I *wanted* to stay with 'that man.'

Back in Dublin, looking shifty, Aidan announced the bursary money had run out. He would be returning to London. To wife and kinder? Indeed. 'We never said the L.O.V.E. word, did we?'

Two days later, manuscript under his oxter, we waited in the departure lounge at Dublin Airport. Aidan went to the loo, leaving his briefcase under a chair. I didn't have the guts to grab his manuscript, in those pre-internet days, his only copy, and run. Goodbye Bornholm Night Ferry! Goodbye sexy, broken English masterpiece!

Dumb with pain, I sat immobile.

Inexplicably, back in Dublin, I decided a trip to Malaga would be fun—an hour's drive from where Aidan and Jill 'and the lads' had had happy and unhappy times, where he had based his other masterpiece, *Balcony of Europe*. Mum agreed to come. Three days in, surrounded by endless memories of Aidan, his 'Balcon de Europa,' remembering the pigeon Spanish we spoke to each other, the goats, the cafes, the horse-drawn carriages, I started to cry. I couldn't stop. I had to get away. Get home. Blundering from airline office to airline office trying to get us an early flight out.

Mum, furious, sat at a cafe table, complimentary wrapped biscuit unopened on a plate beside her: 'This is *ridiculous.'* And 'Are you really going to spoil the entire holiday?'

'I'm falling apart Mum. I need to get home.'

'Tsk!' Mum went. 'Such a fuss about nothing!'

'I *loved* him, Mum.'

'Much good it did you.'

'Mum.'

'Mum!' she aped back in a jeering voice.

The airlines were adamant. 'No es *possible,* Señora!' It was peak tourist season. Nobody had a spare seat for a swollen eyed *gringa.* When we finally boarded our flight home, Mum turned: 'Well, are you happy now?' I was so far from happy I couldn't speak. I pulled down the blind on the oval window and put my sunglasses on. Fuck *off*, Mum, I thought. Sensing my rage, even if it was repressed, as we taxied down the runway Mum said, 'I'm going to buy us both gin and tonics.' Her gesture of reconciliation: I promise I won't tell everyone Rosita spent the entire holiday blubbing.

Years later an almost blind Aidan came to stay with me and the children. The children, now teenagers, intrigued with his insistence we needed six bottles of red wine before heading up to the house, thought he was hilarious. When they had gone upstairs, he leaned on his stick in the doorway. He had something to say. He wanted to apologise. Leaving, all those years ago, he felt 'like a heel.'

'Good.'

3

My book with Pan, *On Our Backs, Sexual Attitudes in a Changing Ireland*, was published.

It was said to 'break new ground.'

To be honest, the ground in Ireland when it came to sex was still mostly concrete. Ignorance, fear and guilt, religious and State repression, decades of physical and sexual abuse, confusion 'medicated' with alcohol, did not make for happy, sensual trysts. Oh no. Reading it now I'm horrified. So much suffering. All so that a patriarchal and clerical elite could ram their hypocrisies down our throats?

In 1979 we were still just at the foothills of the sexual revolution in Ireland, with a long, long way to go.

PART FIVE

'Life is a shipwreck, but we must not forget to sing in the lifeboats.'

Voltaire

1

Staying with a friend in London, I decided to ring J. He immediately dumped the woman he had been with for the past eighteen months and roared home.

He wanted no examinations of the past. No recriminations. *No!* He wanted to tell me morning, noon and night how brilliant I was, how much he had missed my singing, my certainties, the house, Ireland, O *Everything!*

We *had* to get married again. We *had* to go and buy proper gold rings this time. We would show everyone just how in LOVE we were. Okay? Wasn't ours the greatest love story since Richard Burton and Liz Taylor? Since Humphrey Bogart and Lauren Bacall? Wasn't it? Tell me. *Tell me.*

'Don't ever leave me again!' J said, eyes shining with tears. 'Promise me! *Promise* me!'

In a whirl of gold rings, protestations of undying love, buying stuff, I could hardly remember: had I left him? Had he left me?

He had just been offered an assignment in Sri Lanka. We'd have a proper honeymoon there. Playing out the greatest love story ever told, 'the Pearl of the Indian Ocean as backdrop. 'How about *that?'*

I went to visit Mum. She was sitting at the kitchen table, having soup.

'I've got a husband!' I said, showing her the fat new gold band.

Mum looked. Pressed a napkin to her mouth. 'I thought you had a husband.'

'We're doing it all over again!' I said, running water into a jug for the flowers I'd brought. 'Aren't you pleased for me?'

I put the jug and flowers down on the table.

Mum got up. Placed her soup bowl and spoon in the sink.

'I thought you'd be *pleased*!' I said. 'We're going to Sri Lanka!

We'll have a second honeymoon there!'

'That's nice,' Mum said, running water onto her bowl and spoon.

'*Mum!*'

She turned and looked at me. 'What do you expect me to say?'

I snatched up my bag. '*Be* like that then,' I said. 'See if I care!'

I shouted back down the hall before slamming the front door.

Twin Sister, after a couple of glasses, said, 'How come you always run away though, just after you've got a new book out?'

I was so surprised the best I could manage was: 'Run away?'

'It's what you always do,' said Twin Sister, re-filling her glass. 'You never stay and face the music.'

Sorry *what?*

Ignore her, said J., she's just jealous.

2

In Sri Lanka's capital, Colombo, we got a large, second story room in the Galle Face Hotel looking out over the Indian Ocean, the hotel pool, a trembling aquamarine lozenge below the window. We watched the sun, a boiling red ball, wobble and melt into the sea. We ate lobster on the verandah, the sea thumping away at the breakwater below, a band of coconut trees clacking their fronds in the evening breeze. Pole-thin waiters wrapped in white linen aprons down to their feet brought wine, bread, salads, homemade mayonnaise. The air stiff with heat, humidity, sea salt.

Upstairs in a heavy desk drawer a yellowing brochure said Emperor Hirohito had stayed here, and Richard Nixon, and Vivien Leigh, and Mark Twain and Arthur Conan Doyle. And Prince Philip. And Pope John Paul 23rd. 'What the fuck was that old devil doing here?' J. asked looking up from the paper. 'Arthur C. Clarke stayed here,' I said, 'and *wrote* here!'

I pretend-wrote every day at the desk looking out to the acres of rolling blue ocean. I tried writing a children's book. I kept diaries. I wrote out my dreams. Mostly the writing was a way of avoiding painful questions: What am I doing with my life? Why did Aidan leave? What am I doing back with J?

3

We drove from the Galle Face up to the tea plantations and Nuwara Eliya, the 'Hill Station' where the fusty pageantry of colonialism—bungalows, club houses, cricket grounds, survived.

Curling up through the highlands, through the stepped paddy field terraces hugging the hilly curves, passing rickshaws, groaning bullock carts, palm thatched huts, wildly waving children, the road finally stopped at the cool of the plantations.

The old planters in white hats, khaki shorts, sandals with white socks, joshed J. along like a long lost son. He loved it. Playing up to it like anything. 'Aren't they bloody marvellous?' The old buffers with their solar topees, their 'chota' pegs for breakfast, pink gin sundowners at 6 o'clock, angostura bitters for pick-me-ups. Their servants, chauffeurs, gardeners. Their bungalows, cricket grounds, clubs where everyone, white and brown, spoke the colonial lingo: Pukka chap. Quite so Old Boy. Time for a sundowner, Old Sport? Old girl? Absolutely excellent bloody weather for another game of cricket, eh what? My dear fellow. Some chai, Sahib? The club rooms, not just identical to the club rooms of colonial times, but actually the club rooms of colonial times, faintly mouldy, heavy with taxidermied wildlife the Brits had so eagerly slaughtered—elephant, antlered deer, leopard, water buffalo. An elephant's foot topped with brass—as an ashtray.

Along with the Consultants from America, Japan, the UK, who

earned ten, twenty, times their Sri Lankan counterparts, the white Sahibs still held unquestioned power. Were awarded the best bungalows, the largest expenses, the latest four-wheel drive jeeps. From a distance the plantations looked idyllic. Thousands of acres of low green tea bushes, women in brightest pinks, blues, yellows, picking into wicker baskets held by straps around their foreheads, brown arms stretched out to pluck, pluck, pluck.

Surface tranquillity hid ruthless oppression. The workers, mostly Tamil, brought in centuries ago by the British as 'indentured labourers,' still lived in the tin-roofed slums built by the British, with no proper running water, or sewage, electricity for maybe two hours a day, average pay €2, half pay if the quota was not met. Up close you could see the poverty, the exhaustion, the women's skin burnt black, old before their time, grandmothers holding babies, stick figures of despair.

Back in Colombo a departing British couple said we should take their house. One wall entirely glass, with glass doors that rolled stiffly back, faced onto a small river, an Henri Rousseau style jungle. Brilliant kingfishers, as if electrified, shot down from the greenery. Water snakes rolled in the brown water. Iguana the size of large dogs shouldered their way up onto the bank.

The expats said the weed here was fantastic. And incredibly cheap. J. said it was probably impossible to locate. I asked Velhu, our cook, if he knew where I might buy some.

'One moment, Memsahib.' Velhu disappeared, reappeared minutes later, changed from his usual spotlessly white lungi into khaki colonial shorts, khaki shirt, a snap up brown 'slouch hat' from circa WW1. 'I come back immediately, Memsahib' and he set off, a stately dignified figure on a large black bike, proceeding slowly down the middle of the road. Half an hour later he was back, once

again in his spotless lungi. 'I get for you, Memsahib.' In the crown
of his snap-up cap nestled a dozen fat cigars of pungent weed.

'Velhu! That's *fantastic!*'

'Thank you, Memsahib.'

J. and I, inexperienced smokers, rolled up that evening. Within minutes we were falling around laughing, mesmerised by the
translucent geckos, internal organs pulsing, as they ran up the
wall. Running to the kitchen to make massive gin and tonics,
marvelling at the pearls of condensation on their curved glass
surfaces, the streams of bubbles rushing up from the ice cubes, J.
asking 'What will we have? Miles Davis or Ella Fitzgerald?' Miles's
trumpet filling the room.

'Let's do another,' said J.

'Fucking *hell*,' J. said grinning, 'why did no one tell me about
this stuff before?'

We spent the weekend smoking. Eating. Playing music. Going
naked. Marvelling at the kingfishers. The geckos. The jungle lush-
ness outside. Miles on the stereo. Then Ella.

Early Monday morning. J. got a phone call. A consultant from
the UK was visiting, could he come in straight away? He started
banging around his study, gathering up his stuff. Of *course* he
can't now take the bloody day off, get stoned again. Am I *mad?*

He bangs out the door without even a coffee. Velhu, standing
by the table holding the fresh pot, is crestfallen.

'Bwana is very busy, Memsahib?'

'Bwana is an arse.' I say.

'Excuse me, Memsahib?'

'Yes Velhu, Bwana very busy.'

That evening J. came home and went straight to his study. No,
he didn't want to smoke. He was not going to, ever again. It made

him paranoid.

'Don't be daft! You're just *tired*!'

J. closed the solid wood door. 'You heard what I said,' he said from the other side. The house, heavy with silence, slipped back into its dark, closed-up self.

'I am so fucking *bored.*'

'And you're not helping.'

'How am I not helping?'

'You're just not.'

4

Well,' Mum said back in Dublin, 'how are you?'

'Good,' I said.

But how was I really? I was in my thirties. Every manuscript I tried to birth sank, unfinished, into oblivion. I was doing book reviews. And bits of journalism. Going round in circles.

'How is J?' Mum asked.

J. had decided we should buy a cottage in the country. It was December and he wanted to check out a house near the Sally Gap. Okay. By the time we got to Blessington, gateway village to the Wicklow mountains, big lazy flakes of snow were spiralling down, the countryside softly disappearing under enchanting Christmas cake whiteness. We stopped for coffee.

By the time we got to the Sally Gap, road visibility had dropped to a couple of feet. The snow, great pillows of white in the ditches either side, was now a blizzard. 'Shouldn't we go back?'

'No fucking way,' J. said, 'am I turning back now.'

A red face, peaked cap crusted with white, appeared at the car window. J. wound the window down letting the snow rush in.

'Are ye mad?' shouted the face, 'Ye could die on this mountain.

Go *back*!' Radiating fury, J. painfully reversed three miles down to the nearest lay-by.

'Why don't we stop in the village for a bowl of soup, a toasted cheese sandwich, a hot toddy?'

'I'm not fucking hungry' J. snarled. We drove home in silence.

Back at the house, he poured himself a brandy. 'You never fucking let up the whole day, did you?'

'I didn't say *anything*!'

'You never fucking stopped,' J. said, 'you and your fucking negativity.'

He turned suddenly white.

'*Doctor*' he shouted, banging his chest, 'Get a fucking doctor. I'm having a fucking *heart* attack.'

Ten minutes later big burly men, blue scrubs under their bomber jackets, filled the hall: 'So where's the boss man then?' J., helped to a stretcher chair fastened with yellow luggage straps, was lifted up and out to the ambulance, blue lights flashing against the snow. He waved a gloved hand as the doors closed over.

OhMyGod. Is he going to die?

From inside a cubicle a male nurse emerged. 'We're sedating him now. Taking him to a bed. You can go home.'

'Is he—?'

'You can come in the morning,' the nurse said firmly.

'Don't worry,' he said, 'he's in the right place.'

The right place, the right place, the right place to die, my boots hammered out on the icy pavements.

In the morning J. was sitting up in bed having tea. 'How did *you* get in?'

It wasn't a heart attack. It was angina. Brought on by stress. There were drugs he would be on for life. Probably an operation.

No long-term prognosis was possible at this stage.

I rang psychiatrist and friend Ivor Browne. What did he think? It all sounded so frightening. Drugs for life. An operation? Ivor delivered a concise precis of the horrors of lifelong pharmaceutical drug dependency and open heart surgery. 'The future' he said, 'will be you pushing him around in a wheelchair.'

Jesus. Would he speak with J?

I listened in as Ivor boomed down the phone to J. that afternoon: 'You can go down the road of drugs, life-long crippledom, stents, open heart surgery, etc. etc., or you can start to face what you've repressed. Start to deal with it. And go on to live a perfectly healthy, happy life. A happier one than you've probably had for a very long time.'

J. had got a real fright. He agreed to begin sessions with Ivor.

Happiness! J. was going to find out why he was so fucked up! We would have a happy life! Happier than we'd had for a very long time! Hurray! Hurray! HURRAY!

After three sessions Ivor confided he had seldom met anyone 'so completely locked down' as J. Unable to shift anything, he whacked syringes full of ketamine into J.'s thigh. Still nothing! *Not a thing!*

I felt ridiculously relieved. It wasn't just me that couldn't get J. to talk.

One morning, after another session, more ketamine, J. sat up in bed very excited. He'd had a dream! He was on a train track! A huge train was thundering towards him!

He was due to travel again. He would pick up the sessions with Ivor when he got back.

5

The week after J. got back, we found a house in the Wicklow mountains. A stone-built bailiff's lodge, with no electricity, no running water, no phone. We decided to sell up the Dublin house and move, full-time, to the mountains.

J.'s rural boyhood self emerged. He dug a garden. Planted vegetables. Bought books about wildflowers, moths, mushrooms. He cut down the gloomy graveyard trees that blocked the view down the valley. Stacked logs for winter. Bought in a generator. Pulled me outside to hear the cuckoo. See the owl in the forest. To see the fox crossing the grass at dawn, the garden seeming to float in early morning mist. Gorse bushes decorated with spider webs.

One evening, getting ready to go out for a run, this thought arrived: I shouldn't go running. I'm pregnant.

'What's the matter?' J called up. 'Why don't you come down to the fire and finish your wine?'

'Just making a cup of tea,' I squeaked.

'*Tea?*'

J. had another overseas assignment. I drove him to the airport next morning, then rang the gynaecologist. Could I see him straight away?

The doctor opened the door himself. 'Come on then!' he said, taking the stairs in threes.

Hot pee gushed over my hand as I tried to pee *into* the plastic cup, *over* the paper wand. *O God.* 'Alright in there?'

'You're pregnant alright!' he said, smacking his hand down on a leather examination couch. 'Hop up.'

Braced for agony, the IUD from Africa in place for years, I waited. The Doc held up a small, gooey piece of wire. 'There's the culprit!'

'That's *it?*'

'I'm guessing you will want a termination?'

'*No,*' I said.

'No?'

'Definitely no.'

I was afraid to tell J., but in bed together the night he got back, he said, '*Fuck*! Your tits feel amazing.' Then, 'Don't worry. We'll manage.' And there we were: Adam and Eve in our mountain eerie. Thick as thieves. Cooking up a baby.

6

London Sister said she was coming to visit. To check up on her pregnant younger sister? Haha. Very funny. Very London in a Burberry trench coat, hairdresser straight hair, Russell and Bromley loafers.

J. took her for a walk around the garden, to the outhouse we were renovating. I saw them from the kitchen window as I was making the coffee, side by side, noticing how familiar they were with each other. The same height, the same *age*. Like brother and sister? 'Coffee!' I called out through the window.

We'd been invited for dinner. New friends, keen to meet this big sister from London, had invited us. Off we went in the best of form.

After dinner, everyone sitting back, the hostess asked where I was having the baby. I said I had decided to have a home birth. That Twin Sister had had her first baby in hospital and it was absolutely horrendous! They had put her legs up in stirrups! Can you imagine? The worst possible position for a labouring mum! Then fitted an electrode, *with a clamp*, to the little baby's skull because labour was taking so long. 'Imagine sticking a clamp into a baby's skull!' I said, hands across my bump.

Talk stopped around the table.

London Sister did a knowing, grown-up, laugh: 'Of course they don't *actually* put a clamp into the baby's skull.'

Nods of assent, and relief, around the table. 'Oh yes, of course not.' Hahaha!

'They *do*!' I said, hot in the face, 'I was just reading about it yesterday!'

London Sister, smiling, turned to J. 'They really don't.'

'Of course not!' J. agreed, smiling. Everyone began talking again. London Sister lifted her glass, smiled. Looked around.

On the way home J., his face lit by oncoming lights, said: 'Why aren't you talking to your sister? It's *embarrassing*. You're behaving like a kid.'

When he'd gone to bed I found my book downstairs: they *do* fix clamps into a baby's skull. They fucking DO.

While J. was cooking breakfast next morning, London Sister fingered the book I'd left on the table.

'Sheila Kitzinger,' she said, 'isn't she a Socialist?'

'Bloody Trot!' J. said over his shoulder, chivying the eggs in the pan.

'She's a *feminist*,' I said.

'Same difference,' J. laughed.

London Sister smiled. Straightened a table mat with one finger.

J. suggested a drive over to Glendalough. At the hotel, he said, 'Irish coffees all round?'

Yes please!

'You're still drinking?' London Sister said. 'And smoking?'

'Mum drank and smoked, with all of us,' I said, feeling myself going red.

'That was only at the very beginning,' London Sister said. In the voice older ones use when they've just delivered information they know you can't refute.

J. snapped his fingers for the barman. 'One Irish coffee isn't going to hurt her,' he said. 'or the odd joint.'

How did London Sister know Mum had stopped? Had she? London Sister and I were laying the table. 'I'm *starving,*' I said. J. was making beef casserole. A bottle of wine had been opened. The wood fire in the sitting room was a spitting blaze. Nina Simone on the stereo.

'I'm so hungry I could eat a Christian Brother's arse through a slatted chair,' I said.

'What?' said London Sister.

J., laughing, carried the casserole to the table: 'Make way for Christian Brother's arse.'

The night before she was due to go back, I glanced through London Sister's open door. Her city clothes were carefully laid out on the bed: beige cashmere dress, thin leather belt with a gold clasp, Burbery trench with plaid lining, black tights, black patent pumps side by side on the floor. All ready to go back to real life.

Downstairs she was drying her hair in front of the fire. 'How do you manage without a hair dryer?!'

'Oh, it's because of the generator. We can't overload it,' I said. Which was only partly true.

London Sister sat, almost in the fire, rushing her brush down again, again, through thick grey hair. Finally a bandana tied around it so it wouldn't go 'frizzy.' She got up and said, 'Okay,' meaning she was ready for supper.

J. and I drove her to the train. She was going to stay with Mum. Twin Sister rang a couple of days later: 'London Sister says you'd want to watch it. You're in danger of getting really fat.'

7

London Sister and her husband were breaking up.

No!

We all loved London Sister's husband. He was kind. And funny. His eyebrows were life forms of their own. He'd taught us jazz. Miles Davis. Johnny Dankworth. Cleo Lane. South African township music.

J. said I should go over. Talk to London Sister. *Do what I could.*

Eager, foolish do-gooder, I went over, taken aback by a note in J.'s scrawled hand, 'London's greatest lawyer!' pinned on the kitchen wall. London Sister walked in.

We went to the park. What exactly *was* the problem? Had she and her husband, 'the love of her life,' talked? Did she still love him? Did he love her? We walked around the park and back again. London Sister was doing little cries into her handkerchief, but I still had no idea what the problem was. Who wanted to leave who? Why? Why did London Sister say she was heartbroken? Couldn't sleep? Couldn't eat? Why was her lovely husband drinking himself stupid every evening? Alone upstairs? Taking handfuls of antidepressants? Drinking so much that he had to start the day with a freezing shower, out in the *yard?* What was that about? He's on a lot of medication, said London Sister. For what? Depression. What's he sad about? Oh she didn't really know.

The evening before I left, for the 1000th time, I suggested therapy. 'Why not go and *see* someone and try and sort things out?'

Her friend Sue had urged the same thing.

London Sister started full Freudian therapy. On the fifth session something 'came up.' A psychological breakthrough! How *exciting!* London Sister came home, didn't talk to anyone, went to bed and developed a very high fever that didn't let up for ten days. Her sheets were soaked through three times a night. Her husband, a faithful dog, slept on the floor outside the bedroom.

London Sister refused to discuss it. What terrible secret did the therapist retrieve from her unconscious? She wouldn't say. She had cancelled all further sessions.

She'd lost a stone and a half. It didn't seem the right time to say: for fuck sake, just spit it out. What the hell came up? It can't be *that* bad. No. She would not say. Not now. Not ever.

8

Six weeks after our tiny daughter arrived into the world, born upstairs at home, the birds singing as J. came up with tea and whiskey for me and him and our wonderful midwife Ann Kelly, he said he had to travel again. Again to London. Again to stay with London Sister.

Okay.

Twin Sister rang. I sat at the telephone table, the baby, a wobbling hot bottle, on my shoulder.

'Jesus Christ,' Twin Sister went, 'You'll have to get your back teeth in there.'

'How do you mean?'

'I mean he's fucked off and left you with a six-week-old baby! What's he doing over there anyway?'

'Writing up a report,' I said. The words sounded fake even as I said them.

The baby started crying.

'How is she?' asked Twin Sister.

'What?' I said over the baby's cries.

'Your little one! How is she?' said Twin Sister.

I took the baby out for a walk in the new pram. It was what

you were supposed to do: Give a feed. Change the nappy. Put on a new baby-gro. I went through the motions in a haze of exhaustion. Outside a grey overcast sky. The new green corduroy pram ridiculous for the rough mountain track. The baby's little face looked pinched and sad above the tightly tucked blankets and snapped green cover. Everything felt wrong. The grey sky. The stupid pram. Most of all my new daughter's sad pinched little face. Something's so *wrong,* I thought as I turned, and pushed for home, I need to find out what.

On the sofa, the baby in her Moses basket beside me, I lay down. What was it? Was it me? Was it normal? Was it postnatal blues?

Doing the breathing Ivor Browne had shown us—deep breath in, then short sharp breaths out—I started a deep dive. Concentrating. *Concentrate.* Gradually I began to feel myself floating down. Down into a vast deep ocean. Down, down, *down.*

What is wrong *with me? Why am I not feeling mother love?*

I touched bottom.

A calm, clear voice said: *I don't feel anything. I'm in shock.*

I plunged up. Gasping. *What?*

Trembling, I stood in the middle of the room. In the mirror over the fireplace a white face gaped back: *I can't feel anything. I'm in shock.*

Terror then: I'm alone with a tiny baby miles from anywhere, and I'm in shock. I'm *concrete* I'm in shock so deep. How am I going to look after my little one? How am I going to get out of shock? The shocks of unhappiness at home with Mum and Dad. The shock of boarding school. The shock of coming up against J's fuck-off darkness. His leave me fucking alone darkness. His, you are so fucking boring darkness. His furious rejections followed by intense, confusing reconciliations: I was *joking,* silly!

I stared at the mirror. Feeling myself falling back through years, feeling, with horror, the concrete carapace that was me. But who was me? There was no me, just this horrible Jolly Hockey Sticks construct who shouted a lot, drank a lot, argued a lot, drank more, cried. My false self, marching around on stiff legs, giving out.

I started to cry, feeling the tears running down my concrete face. Was I going mad?

The baby started moving in her cot. Face wet, heart pounding, I went to pick her up, as I held her to my heart, I got this terrible plunging realisation: J. and London Sister are having an affair. OF COURSE THEY ARE.

The sword in my heart must have scraped my little one's. She screamed.

I rang Twin Sister.

'There is *definitely* something going on between J. and London Sister.'

A moment's silence. Then, Twin Sister, noisily eating something, sounds of crying, someone hoovering in the background, went into a rant about how Second Eldest Sister had eyed up *her* husband, at her fucking wedding. *At her fucking wedding, for fuck sake!* Anyway, she said, she really had to go. Her husband was calling her. Was I okay?

I rang Ivor. 'Ivor, I think I'm in shock.'

Ivor boomed down the phone, 'O yes, perfectly understandable given the emotional—.'

I made an excuse and put the phone down, it wasn't what I needed. But what did I need? I stood by the phone feeling as if the house, as if everything I knew, had been bombed into rubble. To come out of shock, to come out safely, to keep my little daughter safe, I had to start all over again. This time with truth.

I walked up and down, up and down, the kitchen, patting my little bundle in her sling. Every time I tried to put her down she cried out. Every bone and sinew in my body screamed out with exhaustion. It was morning. The phone rang.

'Hello there!' said J.

'Hi,' I said.

'How's the bundle?'

Our daughter, balanced on my shoulder, began crying.

'Still howling, I hear!' J. laughed.

'She's fine,' I said. 'She's good.'

J. said London Sister knew all about 'quieting' babies. 'I'll hand you over to her,' he said before I could say no. *Please* no.

'Hello,' said London Sister in her creamiest voice. 'Your *husband*,' she said, in that special voice women use when they have stolen your man, 'your *husband*,' said London Sister, 'is standing at the end of my bed with a cup of tea.' Hahaha! I stayed silent. 'He says you're having a lot of trouble with the baby, that she's crying all the time.'

'I'm not,' I said. 'She's fine.'

'I know you're very strict about these things, Zibbie, but all you have to do is buy a soother. Better still, why don't I buy a couple and send them over to you? Honestly, you'll never look back.'

'I don't want a soother for her.'

'Honestly, Zibb—' she started.

'I don't want a soother,' I went, trying to keep the shake out of my voice.

Miffed at this ignoramus who wouldn't accept help from the ever so gracious Queen, London Sister handed me back to J.

Standing in the cold kitchen, the fire unlit, exhausted, the baby heavy as a rock in my arms, I didn't reply to J.'s 'Do what your big sister tells you!' Then, 'Go get a soother you daft eejit!'

I walked and walked, shoosh-shushing the baby, my heart pounding all through me: *I'm in shock. I can't feel anything. I'm in shock.*

Days going by as if on acid. Days coming to terms with being an emotional paraplegic. Everything heightened to a barely bearable degree. Skinless, naked, exhausted I could smell the soot in the chimney. See the impurities in the water coming out of the tap. See into people's minds. See the Collective Unconscious—all of us swimming in the same waters. Every gush of hatred, sarcasm, mistrust adding to the poison. I could feel the slug, picked up off the path, quivering with life. See the clouds of uncertainty passing over my little one's face at my every inward swerve. Feel my milk rushing down to her sucking. Getting up afterwards, my head ringing, thinking I might faint: *How am I going to get us through? How am I going to survive, skinless in this thick skinned world, how? How am I going to get the truth about J. and London Sister out in the open?*

I drove down to the village. The baby in her Moses basket. The country girls behind the shop counter looked up, frightened. 'How's the baby?' The village gossip came over, poked the baby with an enamelled red nail: 'So where is your Daddy young lady?' The country girls exchanged alarmed glances.

Everybody knew.

I drove down to Mum's house. Youngest Sister, home from the UK, rushed in to the sitting room with her camera. Click click click click. Photographic documentation for London Sister? I didn't have the guts to ask. Youngest Sister, Second Youngest Sister, Second Eldest Sister, all wanted to hold my little one. I was afraid handing her over. They seemed like hyenas. Desperate to feast on love. Back up at home, I lay on the bed, the windows dark, my little one at my side. My body felt made of the same stuff as the mattress—coiled springs, air pockets, dried horse hair.

Can you die from tiredness? Can you die from lies?

9

J. came back. I left the baby with him to run downstairs. Have a quick, longed-for bath. When I came back up I found him leaning over her, his voice cold: 'Why are you always crying? What's the *matter* with you?' I ran in and snatched her up.

I tried to tell him about this amazing truth I'd discovered: that I was in shock. How I now had to fight tooth and nail to get out of shock. I *had* to, to become a good Mum. An instinctive Mum, I said. Like a leopardess. Who will tear to absolute fucking shreds anyone who comes near her little ones. J., a straw hat on his head, was sitting up in bed holding a mug of hot tea. He laughed loudly. 'You're a complete fucking savage, you do you know that don't you?'

I couldn't tell him I thought he and London Sister were having an affair. I couldn't. Now that he was back again, I could barely tell myself; the fire was lit, there was food, coffee, a mum, a dad, a baby, a cat, a dog—a family.

Was I going back into shock?

10

London Sister announced she was coming over! A 'Visit the New Baby Trip!' Wouldn't that be fun! She was coming with her husband and her two pre-teen children. And their dog. They would be driving.

J. hurried out to meet the family emerging noisily from their car. Their little dog bustled in, tail up, ears pricked forward, to where our dog was confined to a playpen. The vet said the 'only hope' for mending his damaged back was to keep him quiet. Absolutely no excitement. *No* jumping. London Sister's dog sniffed our boy's empty bed, peed on it, ate the food in his dish, drank his water. Our fellow barked his furious indignation, scrabbled upwards, fell back, yowling.

The baby in my arms, I looked around for J. 'Help?'

'Shut the fuck up, George!' J. shouted.

'Maybe—,' I began.

'Kids,' said J., 'take your dog for a walk. Okay?'

'For fuck sake George!' J. shouted. Then turning to the adults: 'Drinky poos?'

Supper was late. The baby asleep upstairs, arms free, I hurried about setting the table, pouring wine, putting chips and burgers out for the young people. Burgers demolished, the young ones asked to go down to the tv room.

London Sister, cheeks now pink, moved her chair closer to J., sideways on, her knees almost touching his thighs as she laughed up into his face, as J., clearly delighted, wrenched a cork from another bottle.

I glanced at London Sister's husband. Had he noticed? Very slowly London Sister's husband began to fall forward face first into his dinner plate. London Sister leaned across, pulled him upright by the hair. Fish bones, mashed potato, salad leaves plastered onto his face, he stared around: 'Ergomfftrllagmab.'

J. laughed so hard he had tears in his eyes, 'His fucking *face!*'

In the bathroom I sat on the toilet seat, my heart an out of control piston inside its blind chamber: '*She's in love with him. SHE'S IN LOVE WITH HIM!*' Through the roaring of blood in my ears I could dimly hear J. and London Sister's voices in the kitchen, then J. calling out, 'Oi, young one, what are you up to in there?' Reaching behind me, I flushed the loo. The water gushed away and down. As if it would take my insides with it.

As I came back into the kitchen, London Sister's pretty young daughter was standing by a bowl of avocados.

'Can I take one of these?' She held up a pear.

'Of *course* you can!' said London Sister, 'that's what they're there for!' As if she already owned everything: the avocados, the house, J.

'Come 'ere,' said J. 'You look like you've seen a ghost!'

'Mmm.' I did a half smile.

I made excuses. The baby would need feeding soon. I was going to go up to bed. Leaning over our dog's pen, trying to get him to lie down, I heard quick footsteps behind me: 'Still got your big Irish ass!' said London Sister's husband as he kicked. As I almost toppled. As shouts of laughter came from the dinner table.

Upstairs I lay awake in the dark, listening to my little one's breaths. Waves of shock and anger like sheet lightning rushing through me.

In the morning London Sister was already at the sink. 'Good morning!' Her brightest best self in a fresh pink blouse, pressed white jeans. 'Would you like some tea?!' The jolliest, most big sisterly sister.

'Please take off my gloves and apron,' I said.

'What?' She pretend laughed.

'Please take off my things and leave the washing up.'

'*What?*' A little screechy now. Pulling off the gloves, she threw them on the floor, my apron alongside.

Her face flushed, she said, 'You're hardly in a position—,' looking at me, the baby in my arms.

'Thank you,' I said, picking my things off the floor.

London Sister slammed out the door.

A couple of minutes later she was back.

'I suppose you wouldn't *mind,*' she said, voice curdling, 'if I made my *husband* a cup of tea?'

'I wouldn't,' I said. But I stayed standing, watching, holding my little daughter in my arms as she boiled the kettle, clattered cups, milk, sugar onto a tray.

J. cornered me in the kitchen. 'Why aren't you talking to your sister? You're making everyone feel very awkward.' I looked out the opened window. London Sister and her husband, now also in fresh shirt, fresh chinos, were drinking margaritas on the patio, the young ones put on a bus earlier to go visit their cousins in town.

'Come join us!' London Sister's husband waved.

I touched the fluff of our little daughter's black hair, her tiny body warm against mine in her denim baby sling.

'I'm going to go for a walk,' I said, 'get her a little sleep.'

'Okay,' said J., assembling fresh lemons on a wooden board. 'Come back soon though or we'll have drunk everything.' Hahaha!

'At least you'll always have her!' London Sister called out as I started up the mountain path.

11

J.'s young adult son and his punk girlfriend came to stay. She had blonde cornrows. Safety pins in her ears. Torn pink and black tutus worn one on top of the other, black bovver boots. She caused a sensation in the village. 'Is she one of them punks, is she?'

'Why don't you have more mirrors, Zibb?' she asked. 'I like to *see* myself.'

I couldn't think of an answer. Imagine loving yourself enough that you wanted to *see* yourself?

The young people pressed wildflowers. Made daisy chains. Made sketches in their journals. Enjoyed the baby, now a toddling and talking baby. Sitting on a rug in the garden with her, with her red cassette player and nursery rhyme cassettes. The Elves and the Shoemaker. The Twelve Dancing Princesses. The Emperor's New Clothes.

'This is *brilliant* Zibb! I can't wait to have *millions* of babies!'

J's son had cancer. He'd been exposed to Agent Orange on a farm in Australia.

'The farmers use *Agent Orange*?'

'Yup. Apparently it's a brilliant pesticide.' And a brilliant killer, I didn't say. He'd developed Hodgkin's Lymphoma, his once shoulder length hair now a threadbare old man's stubble. His body that awful hollowed out cancer body.

He only alluded to his cancer twice. Once when he was cooking brown rice. I said I could put it on the gas cooker, hurry it up. He said no. The macrobiotic people all said cooking slowly was better for your 'immune.'

The second time was when I was showing him their room. I pushed the wooden shutters closed—'So you can sleep on in the morning.'

'Oh no,' he said, opening them back wide, 'that would remind me of a coffin.'

I tripped leaving the room. Almost going headlong down the stairs.

When the baby was asleep the young people and I smoked weed, sitting out in the garden, the starry starry sky above, thrumming with a million trembling lights. J., on a chair on the kitchen steps, drinking brandy, halloo'ed.

I got pregnant again.

PART SIX

'If you're silent about your pain, they'll kill you and say you enjoyed it'.

Zora Neale Thurston

1

J. was in London. Again at London Sister's. When was he coming home? It had been five weeks. The children and I really *needed* him.

'What is it you actually *want*?' J. said coldly. 'I'm cooking breakfast.'

Sounds of a kettle building to a boil.

I moved the baby from one hip to the other. 'I, I don't know what's going on.'

As if the answer had been ready made earlier, J. shot back, '*I* do.'

In the background I heard the toaster popping, then J. saying, 'I've told another woman that I love her.'

The floor swayed. I heard a cry, '*Mum!*'

'Are you there?' asked J. 'I'll be coming home at the weekend to collect my stuff.'

2

J. said he and the woman, who wasn't London Sister, oh no, but one he had lived with before. Now married, with a daughter. She and J., he said, had sat in her car. 'For hours and hours.' Telling each other how much they loved each other. That they had always loved each other. That now they must *do* something about it.

Meantime, I was *not* to ring her. She would be away for four weeks. And 'uncontactable.' He would be away also. Also 'uncontactable.'

Hmm. All very strange.

J. arrived four days later. A brutally short new haircut, a new suit, new briefcase, new overnight bag, my little daughter, who had run, whooping, to her Dad, was in his arms.

'Give us a kiss then,' he said, advancing. I swerved away. 'Oh, it's going to be like that is it?'

115

Making supper—normal life unbearably stretched over the broken bones of the cataclysm—J. mentioned a friend who'd also left his wife: 'His psychiatrist told him he was not obliged to stay with someone so depressed. He was not obliged to sacrifice his life for a wife who was mentally sick.'

Fuck, I though. So *that's* the line. Did the clever psychiatrist have anything to say about the children left behind with this very depressed, very sick mother? Apparently not.

The children asleep, I went to the wardrobe. Pulled out my brightest, best clothes. I was NOT going to accept the allotted role of Mentally Sick, Very Depressed Wife. *No.*

Downstairs J. had built up the fire, flames rushing up the chimney throat. He patted the empty space beside him on the sofa. 'Come *sit.*' I sat on the edge of the table, holding a glass of wine. He was already on his third, he said, and I should get a couple into me. 'Drink up! Wind down! Relax!'

As he was pouring I took a quick sideways look at him. Who *was* this stranger? This used car salesman with a receding hairline, a paunch I hadn't noticed before now straining at his shirt buttons? The Wizard of Oz, minus cloak and wand, revealed as shabby fraud?

Next morning, J. lay in a bubble bath, eyes glistening, hand clasped firmly around an erection, 'It's going to be hard to choose you know!' he said, grinning up from his carpet of winking bubbles.

Hard to *choose*? I stepped backwards, onto a bar of wet soap. J. laughed loudly: 'You almost went arse over tit there, Missus!'

In the kitchen I pulled the baby out of his high chair, shaking the jingling safety harness off his legs, as my little daughter, alarmed, stood up.

'Where are we going, Mum?'

'To the, uh, village. We need some, eh, bread. Um, something for lunch.' Bucketing along the narrow road, the sheep shoving their way frantically through the gaps in the ditches, all dainty clicking feet, cumbersome winter coats, and loud baa-ing, as the little jeep, spitting stones, accelerated around the bend, my daughter standing in the gap between the seats, asking: 'Are you crying because of Dad, Mum?'

It was lunchtime, our little daughter on his left, the baby in his high chair on his right. J. at the table looked up, a heaped forkful of pasta midway between plate and mouth. 'Bring us down some bread love, would you?' he called out. Bending down to get the bread, I heard him, dreamy-voiced: 'She responds to the *lightest* touch on the reins.' At the table, French stick now in hand, J. said: 'I'm going to exercise my prerogative here. I'm going to *stay*!'

'What Dad?' said our little daughter trying to twirl the pasta onto her fork, like her big clever Dad.

'Dad is going to *stay*!' J. said, 'Here! With you and Mum and the baby! Isn't that great news?'

He turned to me. 'Well, are you pleased Missus? Are you?'

I scooped the baby's scattered pasta back into his bowl, mopped at his chin with his towelling bib—'Tuesday' in curling letters embroidered across it.

'Well?' J. urged leaning over to refill my glass, 'are you or are you not delighted with yourself and your delightful husband?'

Suddenly he was all business. O it was hugs and kisses, and, We must go shopping! Let's get this place stocked up with some decent booze and food! Leaning back to pat me on the hindquarters as I walked past: 'You need some condition on you, Missus! You look like something out of Belsen.'

'Yes, well—'

'Yes,well what?' J. wanted to know. Absolutely thrilled with

117

everyone and everything.

He said he was going to take his family on a holiday. Somewhere with some goddam sunshine. Good food. A swimming pool. Nannies for the children. Wouldn't that be the business? Wouldn't it? 'Sun, sex, sea, sand! Don't say you're not gagging for it, Zibb! Hey? Hey?'

I sipped the wine. Edged my way from one jagged second to the next.

That night, J. lit a massive fire.

'Isn't that a bit much? We're a long way from—'

J. laughed. 'You're so uptight these days!'

In the polished bulge of my glass, I saw flames—vermillion, green, blue, sulphurous yellow—rushing up the black chimney throat, the logs crackling and hissing.

J.'s five days were almost over.

Mr. Delighted-with-Himself, Mrs. Belsen, and their two very small children had been invited out. Off they were to go to visit friends. A British, ex-army man and his lovely wife.

Talk. Wine. Joints. Music. Coffee. More wine. More Talk. Brandy. Seated either side of an open fire, I heard J. and our host: 'Something, something, something, bourgeois, middle-class notions of marriage!' followed by a bark of laughter. I felt a shiver of fear.

On the drive home, Mr. Delighted-with-Himself had suddenly transformed back into J. Icy, monosyllabic, foul tempered, hands on the steering wheel, he yanked the car up through the gears as we climbed the hill towards the Pass, hurtled it forward into the blackness on the far side, boot to the floor. 'No I do not want to talk. What the hell is there to talk about anyway?'

'Our marriage?'

'Our *marriage?*' J. snorted, accelerating into the enveloping dark.

In the morning, I stood in the doorway of his study. He was clearing out his papers. Yes, he was leaving. Yes, tomorrow. Just like that? Yes. Just like that. He was booked on the eleven am flight.

'What about *I'm going to exercise my prerogative here? I'm going to stay?'* I tried to keep my voice level.

J. looked up, a bitter sneer across his face. 'It helped pass the time, didn't it?'

I stared.

J. shrugged his shoulders. 'I've changed my mind.'

'You *can't* do this, J. You can't do this to our *children.'*

He looked over his shoulder. 'They'll survive,' he said.

'You're forcing them to go through their whole life without their Dad! Their lives have only just started, and you're walking out,' I cried.

J. looked up, mouth hooked down at the sides. 'If you had half a chance you would too.' He scooped a pile of unused green folders into a box, clapping the lid to.

'*Leave* the children?'

He looked briefly around. 'Leave the whole bloody lot.'

I turned to go, turned back, 'You're their *Dad,* J.'

He turned around. 'Yes, and God help them, you're their mother.'

Trembling, I poured a whiskey, J. going backwards and forwards past the window, carrying folders, files, cardboard boxes. Our little daughter, white-faced, her bottom lip rubbed raw, had climbed into one of the empty cardboard boxes on the kitchen floor, holding her doll, singing, 'The Dad and the Mum are fighting. The Mum is crying. The little girl is holding Vinegar. Vinegar says not to cry.' The baby, his face streaked with rusk and yoghurt, arms up, wailed to be lifted out of his chair.

The endless day was almost over. The children asleep. J., upstairs, lay fully dressed on the bed, reading a thick paperback, a glass of whiskey on the bedside table. 'Not half as good as it thinks it is,' he said, holding up the book, looking at me over his glasses. As if everything was completely normal. Dad reads book. Drinks whiskey. Mum puts babies to bed, pops in to say, Hi. Day is done. Night is here. All is well.

Downstairs, I slipped into J.'s study, easing the door shut behind me. Holding a scrap of paper sideways under the desk lamp, the receiver clamped between ear and shoulder, I dialled London.

'Hello,' I said, my hand cupping the mouthpiece, keeping my voice as low as I could. 'Could I speak to Peter please?'

A cautious, male voice was just saying, 'Who is this—?' when I heard a thundering on the stairs.

J. exploded into the room. 'You fucking *bitch*!' he yelled seizing the phone, savagely jerking the phone wires out from the socket on the wall. 'You fucking *cunt*.'

'I have a right to—'

J. whirled, 'You have *nothing*,' he shouted, stamping on the phone. 'No-thing.' He flung the remains of the phone, its wires dangling, into the corner.

'This is the very fucking last you'll ever see of me,' he said, standing at the door, chunks of plaster spattering onto the floor behind him.

An hour later, he was still outside in the car.

Bare feet pushed into boots, a coat over my nightdress, I walked cautiously out into the freezing blackness. A huge emptiness all around lit by the moon, the stars, in their millions, tiny chunks of glittering glass in the vast, blue-black sky. J. was just visible through the fugged-up windows.

'You'd better come in,' I said. 'You'll catch your death out here.'

He hurried in. Standing at the far side of the bed, a shivering laughing schoolboy, furiously pulling off his clothes, dropping them on the floor he said: 'I hope I'm right in thinking what you brought me back in here for!' then jammed himself in alongside me, his feet ice, his body locked around, all caution now gone with the wind, telling me which of my women friends he'd like to 'frigg': Noeleen, (now there's a waste of a beautiful woman!). Morna, (mainly to annoy her husband! hahaha), Sally *(obviously!).*' He'd like to frigg , and he'd like to frigg—

My voice coming from very far away. 'And are you "frigging" London Sister?'

'I've been frigging her for years and years!' J. said triumphantly. 'She loves it!' Then, as a sober afterthought, 'But she doesn't like cock because she's very cold and controlled.'

The terrible words flying through the air like a blizzard of knives.

A few minutes later I heard J. snoring. On his side snuffling happily. Next door I could hear my little daughter twisting in her bed; the baby, coughing. Outside, in the dark, a vixen let out a series of strangled, banshee wails, a pause, then responding high decibel shrieks from a sister fox the other side of the valley. A farm dog barked its alarm.

The last thing I heard was the grandfather clock beginning its long corkscrew wind up to the sounding of the hour. Then I was gone.

The next morning, J. sat up in bed on plumped pillows, handsome as a film star, confidently awaiting morning tea. 'Where's my tea?'

Downstairs, in the chaos from the night before—dirty plates, empty bottles, piles of clothes, mountains of damp laundry, toys scattered across the floor, the baby in his high chair mashing milk-sodden rusk into the corners of his tray, my little daughter picking currants from her bowl of muesli, arranging them, dripping with milk, onto the table—I tried to think. Think. *Think* for godsakes.

'Where's Dad?' asked my little daughter.

The phone rang. It was Ivor Browne. 'Juno said you'd rung?'

I cupped my hand around the mouthpiece, turning away from the children. 'Last night—,' I began.

Ivor listened intently. 'So. There is *something* going on.' He paused. 'Though, this *could* be some kind of psychological torture.'

From upstairs came a vigorous rat-ata- tat!

'Dad wants his tea,' my little daughter said delightedly, 'He's banging on baby's drum!'

'Mum!' she said, 'Dad's calling you!'

'I'll have to go.'

From upstairs I could hear J. shouting, 'I. WANT. MY. TEA!'

The phone rang again.

It was Twin Sister. 'Hi there. You were looking for me?'

I cupped my hand around the mouthpiece: 'Last night J. told me he'd been, eh, "frigging" London Sister, for years and years—'

A stunned silence. At first, it was as if Twin Sister couldn't hear properly, but when I said the words again, she cried out as if someone had stabbed her. 'Jesus *Christ!*'

'My TEA!' yelled J. from upstairs.

Delighted, the baby was now going ratatat-tat on his tray, specks of milky rusk flying off his spoon.

I made one more call. 'Libs?'

'Yeah?' said a sleepy voice.

'Could I ask you the most enormous favour?'

'Okay.'

'Could you run down to Jim and ask him to come up to me. There's a bit of an emergency going on here—'

I put the big black receiver down and turned to the children.

'Why did you ask Jim to come up, Mum?' asked my little daughter.

I took the baby's bottle to clean it, saying to her, 'So he can see what's going on. Like a witness.' I was at the sink, rinsing rusk off the bottle, when, simultaneously, my little daughter asked, 'What's a witness, Mum?' The phone rang, and I heard a car turn into the yard.

There was furious scrabbling upstairs as J. realised something was afoot. His script—'Tut, tut, are you *mad*? I was *joking* silly!'—was not being adhered to, and an outsider, a fucking *outsider*, had been called in.

He kicked open the door to the kitchen, radiating icy fury. Slamming an unwashed cup into the already choking sink, new briefcase under his arm, he hissed: 'You've really fucked up this time, Zibb.'

I opened my mouth to say something, when our neighbour, stiff with embarrassment, appeared in the doorway, 'Ye were looking for me?'

'I wasn't,' J. said, looking him up and down. 'Maybe *she* was.' J. indicated me with a jerk of his head, then turned, crashing the front door closed after him.

I seized the baby out of his high chair, said to our neighbour, 'I'll be back in a minute,' and ran out after him.

'Where are we going, Mum?' my little daughter asked, hurrying alongside.

'To see Dad off,' I said, thinking I am *not* going to sit inside while he abandons us.

J. was already at the car door when we appeared.

'Where is Dad going, Mum?'

J. started up the engine, reversed, then pulled off in a hail of gravel and exhaust smoke.

In a screech of gears, the big black car tore open the sleepy morning silence of low hills, huge sky, silky blue sea in the distance, sloping green fields and thick furze hedges. The smell of exhaust hanging in the air after the car had disappeared. J. didn't once look back.

The world seemed suddenly, emptily, enormous.

'Don't cry, Mum,' my little daughter said, squeezing my hand, looking up into my face, 'Dad'll be back.'

3

I drove fast into town, the children and I in discordant, ill-matched clothes. Already refugees.

They'd have to listen now! Herewith, please find at last, AT LONG *FUCKING* LAST! incontrovertible evidence, from the horse's mouth, as to the existence of a long-standing, and long-standingly vigorously denied by all parties, sexual relationship, between my husband J., and our eldest sister!

It's true! I was right all along! They've been at it hammer and tongs! FOR YEARS AND YEARS!

I imagined glorious responses: Close ranks! Call the lawyers! Call the cops! Call the men of the family! This is horrific! This is unbelievable! He couldn't be. *She* couldn't be. How could they be? Good heavens! They *are*! You come here darling and live with us, you and your darling little children, and don't you worry about a thing! We will get the best divorce lawyer in the universe to go to war on behalf of you, and your babies! As for those two, those adulterous, those incestuous, family destroying bastard and bitch, they shall be hurled into the seventh deepest hole of Hell—for all Eternity.

FOR ALL ETERNITY!

Long live the truth! Long live the family!

Second Eldest Sister stood in her kitchen, one hand resting on her scratched, see-through jug kettle, coldly inquiring, 'Tea?'

'I've got something pretty weird to tell you,' I began, balancing the baby on my lap as I struggled to roll a cigarette.

Second Eldest Sister gave me a sharp look, watching sideways as I shifted the baby to the centre of my lap, trying to re-lick the edge of the now sodden cigarette paper, tobacco scattering on the table. My little daughter took out her colouring book.

Second Eldest Sister poured boiling water. Quickly, before I lost my nerve, I got up and stood by her, the baby in my arms.

'Last night,' I began, 'J. said, and I quote: I've been frigging London Sister for years and years and she loves it, she screams and—'

For a moment Second Eldest Sister stared, slack jawed, as if Hell, roaring and boiling, had been opened at her feet, *'What?'*

'Stop!' Second Eldest Sister choked out, 'It's, it's *horrible.'*

My little daughter's head came up from her drawing book, 'What's horrible, Mum?'

Second Eldest Sister looked quickly at me: 'Have you told anyone else?'

'I, umm, rang Ivor Browne,' I said, immediately wishing I hadn't.

Second Eldest Sister gave me a you-would-have-to-wouldn't-you? look. 'Well, what did Ivor say?'

'He said,' I said hesitantly, 'there's definitely something going on.'

Second Eldest Sister raised an eyebrow.

'And, oh yes,' I rushed on, 'he said, it could be some kind of psychological torture.'

Second Eldest Sister got busy with a tray, mugs, milk jug, teapot, manipulating the square novelty teapot lid into place. She grasped the tray, 'So, It's psychological torture, eh?'

'He said it *might* be psychological torture.'

'So J. pretends to be madly in love with someone else, then you get jealous,' she stirred the brewing tea vigorously. 'That's how a relationship like yours works, doesn't it? I mean it's the oldest trick in the book!'

'What book, Mum?' asked my little daughter.

I was thinking, *Is* it? *Has* he?

'It's just a saying, Darl,' I said quickly. 'Tell you in a minute.' Then, going over to her, 'Look at your lovely colouring!'

'My God!' Second Eldest Sister exclaimed to my back. 'Is that the time!'

'Is it time to go and see Granny, Mum?' asked my little daughter.

'You haven't told Mum, have you?' Second Eldest Sister said.

I did a screechy laugh, 'Of *course* not!'

She stood, arms over her chest, waiting for us to go. 'Sorry about the tea,' she called after us in a voice that didn't sound sorry. I fumbled the baby into his car seat.

'Hullo everyone,' I pitched through the big hall door of Mum's house twenty minutes later, baby on hip, little daughter at my side,

'There's no need to shout,' said Mum's voice from the sitting room. 'I'm in here'

Sitting in her chair by the fire, a book in her lap, she looked up. I came to a halt in the middle of the room.

'Well,' Mum said, 'aren't you going to sit down?'

'Dad has left us, Granny,' my little daughter said. She turned to look up at me 'Hasn't he, Mum?'

Mum looked across disapprovingly at me.

'Well,' I said, my voice a schoolgirl's squeak, 'he has actually.'

'Hmmm,' Mum went, eyeing my daughter.

'He told Mum,' my little daughter went on, 'that he's never coming back. Didn't he, Mum?'

'He left at nine this morning,' I said in the same awful schoolgirl squeak.

'He's going abroad to work, isn't he?' Mum said. 'Isn't that right?'

I tried to remember if I'd said anything to Mum about J. going abroad.

'Yes,' I said slowly, sitting down heavily, the baby in my arms, opposite Mum. 'He is going abroad.'

'Well then,' Mum said, 'you'll see him when he gets back.'

'He's *gone*,' I said, my voice rising, the baby twisting in my arms. 'He's walked out. Left us. He said…,' I paused and began to yank off the baby's sodden dungarees, 'He *said*....'

Mum, smoothing her skirt, watched. Waited.

'He said…,' I began again, hauling on the baby's pee-logged nappy as he twisted like a fish.

'Anyway,' Mum interrupted. 'I really don't think you should be discussing all this here.' She looked meaningfully across at my little daughter. 'In front of *certain people*.'

I ignored her look. Plunged on. 'He's left us with nothing, Mum. Like I've got sixty quid in my purse. That's *it.*'

'I so dislike that sloppy way of talking.' Mum put on a mock common accent, 'Like dis, like dat, you know like.'

'Anyway,' I said reddening, bent over the baby, 'it's not about money.'

'So what is it about?'

I wanted to yell.

FOR FUCK'S SAKE MUM! You *know* bloody well what it's about. I've been screaming about it for fucking *years*.

Mum waited. 'Well?'

Bunched over, the baby's legs in one hand, manipulating a new nappy under him with the other, I mumbled: 'It's about right and wrong.'

'Hhmm,' went Mum.

I got up.

Attempting to make her voice a bit nicer, Mum said there was coffee in the kitchen if I'd like. 'And orange juice for the children,' she called out as I went down the hall.

Second Youngest Sister was at the kitchen table diagonally slicing rounds of French baguette.

'Hi,' I said.

'Hullo.' She looked up briefly. Silence as she continued to slice.

'Can I ask you something?' I blurted out. 'Do *you* know what's going on?'

She surveyed me, standing in the doorway, the baby on my hip, my little daughter standing beside me.

'No,' she said. She touched the back of her hand to her nose, rubbing it vigorously, knife still in hand. She began slicing again. 'More to the *point*,' she went on, throwing slices into a waiting wicker basket, 'I don't *want* to know.'

She paused. 'Listen—,' she began.

'*Mum,*' my little daughter went, pulling at my jumper.

I lifted the baby and wedged him onto my other hip. 'Last night, J. *told* me. He said he and London Sister are—'

Breadknife in hand, voice loud now, Second Youngest sister said: ' Don't you get it? It's all in your *head*.' She tapped the side of her own head. 'Do you think I don't remember what it was like having a baby that age?' She pointed the bread knife at the baby. 'It's called extreme over-sensitivity from sleep deprivation. It's called being paranoid. PA-RA-NOY-AH,' spelling out the letters in big slicing arcs in the air with the knife.

'Just last night—' I began again.

My little daughter pulled harder, 'Let's *go*, Mum. Mum, I want to *go*—'

'Look,' Second Youngest Sister went, wagging knife now pointed at my little daughter, 'you're freaking out your daughter.'

'*Mum.*'

'Take your kids home,' Second Youngest said. 'Feed them. Read them stories. Whatever it is you do.' She licked mayonnaise off her thumb. 'And stop fantasising about your bloody husband and London Sister.'

I turned and made blindly for the passage, my little daughter running beside me. Second Youngest Sister's voice called up the passage: 'And leave Mum out of it. Do you hear? She's not up for this sort of high volume, emotional crapology.'

'What's happening?' Mum called out from the sitting room. 'Aren't you going to have your coffee?'

'Nothing's wrong, Mother,' Second Youngest Sister shouted. 'She's just leaving.'

'What about the children? Aren't you going to give them something?' Mum called.

'Some other time.' I scrabbled at the front door.

When the children were in bed I decided to try ringing the 'Other Woman.' Again her husband answered. Again the phone was snatched away. A tough, angry English woman's voice shouted : 'Just what is going on?' Holding the receiver tight, I listened, heart walloping, as this 'love of J.'s life' said of course she wasn't going to go and live with him! Who was telling me these things, she would like to know? It was extremely cruel. J. had come round for lunch three weeks previously but that was it. And yes, she added, she didn't love her husband in the 'in love' sense but they 'got on' and were both committed to raising their daughter together. Was that clear?

Sort of, I said, my mouth dry, feeling a stab of pity for the unfortunate husband not loved in the 'in love' sense. Hoping he wasn't listening.

'Did you really ring that woman?' Mum asked. 'Have you no pride?'

'I rang her husband,' I said, 'she snatched the phone. I thought if he's about to be dumped and I'm about to be dumped we should compare notes.'

'It's all so fussy,' said Mum.

It was only after I drove home that it dawned on that Second Eldest Sister couldn't wait to get us out of our house so that she could forewarn the others. Rosita *knows*. She's *coming*.

4

Twin Sister came to visit. She stood in the middle of the kitchen, her dark haired, creamy skinned baby, the living image of his Da, on her hip, licking her fingers noisily, saying loudly the whole situation was absolutely bloody ridiculous. 'They can't expect you to go on living like a walled up widow,' she said, as she threw the baby's licked-clean spoon, into the sink.

'Sorry?' I said weakly, sitting down, my little daughter on my knee.

'We have this plan,' Twin Sister went on, drinking off the baby's orange juice. 'Okay?' She threw the beaker into the sink after the spoon.

'Mum,' my little daughter said, twisting around to look up at me, 'I'm *hungry*.'

Over a pan of sausages, rashers, mushrooms, tomatoes, Twin Sister outlined her and her husband's plan: 'Get the whole family together, right? London Sister included, okay? And 'out' the truth.'

'Well,' I said cautiously, 'I suppose—'

'Put London Sister on the bloody spot, right?' went on Twin Sister, shoving bread into the toaster. 'Is she having an affair with your husband or is she bloody not?'

'What *fair* Mum?' my little daughter asked.

'London Sister couldn't lie in front of the whole family, in front of Mum. Obviously, it would all have to be done in the presence of an experienced counsellor or shrink. Ivor Browne could do it, couldn't he?'

It was almost midnight when Twin Sister headed home in a maelstrom of nappies, borrowed clothes, recipes she'd torn from the Sunday paper, cuttings from the garden, the baby asleep in a rolled up blanket. 'Chin up, hey?' She would start ringing everybody tomorrow. 'We'll get this thing *sorted*.'

She rang two days later. 'They say you're mad, that you're just jealous.'

'Sorry, what?' I fielded the baby as he headed for the patio steps.

'They're saying it's a ridiculous idea,' she went on. 'That they're all working.'

'And they're all furious about Ivor Browne. They say who the hell is he to come barging into our family telling us what to do.'

'O God.'

A week passed. Twin Sister rang again. There was no *way* London Sister was coming over. She was actually incredibly busy. She was her law firm's specialist on women's rights, especially women's rights within marriage. There was no way she could even take an afternoon off at the moment, never mind two whole days, to come over here and defend herself against these ridiculous rumours being spread by her out of control younger sister.

'London Sister actually said that?'

'Said what?' Twin Sister asked.

'I mean the *irony* of it—'

'I'm actually going to have to go,' Twin Sister said. 'We're out the door with work here.'

Quite suddenly, two days later, London Sister, fearless defender of the rights of women, said, well yes, she could come. Just for the day.

'So, she *is* coming?' I asked.

'Yes. She is.'

'Gosh.'

The night before the meeting, I stood in front of the mirror in the sitting room. How would I break through the script? The script of: of *course* I'm not having an affair with your husband! Don't be silly! You're mad!

Then it hit me: it wouldn't be something I would say. It would be something I would have to *do*. And I wouldn't know what it was until the moment came to do it.

5

The morning of the meeting arrived. Twin Sister and I left our children with a babysitter at Mum's house. After Twin Sister had gone to the car, Mum confronted me on the front steps: 'Have you any idea what you're doing to this family?'

I gaped into her cold, angry face.

'What *I'm* doing?'

'Tsssk,' Mum went and clapped the door to.

In the car, still shaking, I said, 'You will not *believe* what Mum just said to me,' yanking the car out into the road.

'*Jesus!!*' yelled Twin Sister as a massive black car barreled past, horn blaring.

'Jesus is right,' I said, flipping the bird at the disappearing limo.

Ivor had secured an oblong room—bare, narrow windows too high and too narrow to climb out of, grey plastic chairs arranged in a horshoe, and a one-way observation window for other shrinks to look in at the mad people, at the far end. All very 'One Flew Over the Cuckoo's Nest.'

London Sister, who'd been met at the airport and taken for a hotel breakfast by Second Eldest Sister, Second Youngest Sister, and Youngest Sister, was dressed in expensive, lawyer black—black cashmere sweater, black expensive slacks, black patent leather shoes, black wool jacket looped over the back of her chair, her hair freshly cut and blow-dried, a pleasant smile taped carefully into place. She sat at the top. Sweetly and politely smiling. Knees politely together, hands in lap. A good girl. The *goodest* of good girls.

Ivor began. He hoped everyone knew why we were all here. Yes? An outbreak of throat clearing, nodding, exchanges of knowing looks. *Good*, said Ivor. What he hoped for was honesty, and understanding. More shifting in chairs, coughing, nodding. Okay? Are we all clear?

A sudden outbreak of shouting: Rosita's mad! Rosita is just jealous! It's all in Rosita's head!

Ivor raised his hand. 'Just a minute! Just a minute *please!* There are actually legitimate questions to be asked here: What is J. up to? What is London Sister up to? Is she allowing herself to be used by J? Is she using him? Very importantly, what is the role of the family here?'

Twin Sister cleared her throat. She said in a quiet voice she didn't know for certain if the affair between London Sister and J. was sexual or not, but London Sister, in supporting J. in deserting me and the children, was totally wrong.

Ivor said he was first going to go around and ask each person if they've slept with J. A second chorus of angry voices. 'This is totally ridiculous!' 'It's all in her *head!*' 'She said herself it's just psychological torture!.'

'Well she's the one with the husband with all the money,' said Youngest Sister. There's an awkward silence, into which Second Youngest Sister announced: 'Frigging is finger fucking.'

Ivor came to Twin Sister. Has she slept with J? Her voice a whisper, her head down, Twin Sister said she had, yes. A long time ago.

'Anyone else?' Ivor asked. Hoots of derision.

Ivor turned to London Sister. 'So, would you say you have a close relationship with J?'

'O *yes,*' London Sister gushed, leaning forward. '*Definitely!*'

Second Eldest Sister looked at the ground. Twin Sister chewed her lip. London Sister plunged on excitedly. She and J. had known each other, oh for years and years! They were like brother and sister! She had known him, *in fact*—here she looked critically across at me—'Oh, long before Rosita did!'

'I am probably closer to J. than anyone else in the family!' she beamed. She paused; earnest, delighted, pink. In *reality*' a little frown had appeared, J. came to her to *rest*. He *needed* rest. He needed *looking after.* Eyes moistly glistening, she looked disapprovingly across at me.

Ivor shifted, re-crossed his legs, coughed, and said: 'So would you say that your relationship with J. is, eh, like a mother-son relationship?'

London Sister pitched towards him eagerly, 'Yes!' she said, flushing an ever warmer pink, 'Yes it *is.* I—'

Go! shouted a voice inside my head.

Jumping up, I sprinted across the room and leapt on top of London Sister, grasping up fistfuls of freshly washed hair.

'Ow,' London Sister squealed, her hands up to her head, 'Ow. Ow. *Ow!*'

Second Eldest Sister, Second Youngest Sister and Youngest Sister rushed forward, screaming: 'You *bitch!*', 'You cow!', ''Let her *go,* Rosita!'

London Sister, in the centre of the melee, was strangely passive.

Ivor, on his feet, shouted: 'Stop this now! Stop this, *immediately!* or I'm cancelling everything.'

I disentangled, elbowed my way out of the scrum and returned, legs trembling, to my seat.

There was a tap on the door. Mum was shown in. After Ivor welcomed her, he began asking her about how things had been in the family after Dad's death, Had they—?

Coolly, Mum replied: 'I thought this meeting was about some silly misunderstanding about a supposed *relationship* between my eldest daughter and—'

Quivering with shame and rage, I shouted: 'You mean the *incest* relationship—'

There was an explosion of shouts, screams, jeers.

'Don't be ridiculous!'

'You are sick!'

'IT IS NOT FUCKING INCEST!'

'Why do you always—?'

'Look it up in the bloody dictionary!'

'Just shut UP! Shut *up*! Okay?'

Finally, it was over. Ivor waited behind. 'You did very well.'

'Really?'

'Yes, really.'

Warmed by Ivor's praise, I made for the Ladies in the basement and came face to face with London Sister. She leaned forward, hissing into my face: 'You don't have ONE OUNCE of compassion. Not an *ounce*.' It was so unexpected I couldn't think of anything to say back as she banged out of the Ladies, Second Eldest Sister in tow.

On the pavement outside, Twin Sister fussed. 'Why don't you and I just go and get coffee?'

'*No*,' I said. 'I'm going to the family lunch. There's *still* been nothing said!'

By the time the babysitter, the children, Twin Sister and I got back to the restaurant, everyone was on their main course. London Sister, lodged between Mum and Second Eldest Sister, began to cry. Her head bowed over her pasta, she sobbed, 'I can't *bear* it. Zibbie looks so *exhausted*.'

I wanted to laugh. It was a laugh, wasn't it? Second Youngest Sister and Second Eldest Sister tut-tutted ostentatiously around her, throwing me dirty looks: how could I be so horrible to poor darling (sobbing) London Sister? How could I be such a *bitch?*

The meal over, all tears gone, London Sister threaded her arm through Mum's and moved swiftly off across the cobbled plaza, Mum in tow. On a sudden impulse I put my little daughter's hand into Twin Sister's and ran after them.

'Hey!' I called out.

London Sister turned. Paused. Drew herself up. 'Yes?'

I shrank to a stop. London Sister, now eighteen feet tall, white, ice cold, dazzlingly beautiful, encased in a long, expensive, dark wool coat, an exquisite fur hat, the soft hairs of fur spiking out in a halo around her perfectly moisturised face, all accoutrements aromatically armoured inside a cloud of exotic perfume, asked: *'Yes?'*

Mum watched, as head down, I muttered, 'Goodbye so.'

'Good bye,' replied the Ice Queen, staring coldly down at this ridiculous excuse for a human being rooted to the cobbles. This pathetic, insect-like, speechless unperson, shivering inside her clothes, holding her none too clean looking baby.

As they left, Mum looked back briefly at me, standing alone in the middle of the plaza, turning to stone, the baby in my arms.

I tore up home. Charged into the house, the baby under my arm, made for the phone. Shaking, I punched in the numbers, as the baby wriggled.

At the other end of the phone, a polite, crisp voice said, 'The Times here, can I help you?'

I grasped the phone tighter, 'What would it cost to place a personal advertisement, premium space, in its own box, in tomorrow's paper?'

There was a flurry at the other end of the line, then 'If I can just take your name and address, Madam....'

Twin Sister hurried in. 'What are you *doing?*'

Twisting away, I began to read into the phone from the scrap of paper I'd written on: 'To whom it may concern. I would like to announce that I am divorcing my husband and citing my eldest sister as co-respondent. I would also like to name my mother, and all the other members of my family, as being parties to the affair, with the exception of my Twin Sister.'

'That's it,' I said into the phone, my jaw so tense I could hardly get it to move. Silence at the other end, then a throat clearing, then, 'If you could just give me a moment, Madam?'

Twin Sister pressed forward. 'You *can't* do this! You don't even know that it's true!'

'Of course it's true,' I shouted. 'Just look at London Sister's face!'

'You can't destroy somebody's whole character because of what you've seen on their face!'

I jerked away. A different, male voice was on the line.

'You were in touch with us just now, Madam?'

'Yes.'

'I'm very sorry,' the voice went, 'but I'm afraid we won't be able to take your advertisement.'

'Um, why?'

'We can't carry advertisements like this. I'm sure you understand. We could face legal action.'

'Maybe it's just as well,' Twin Sister mollified when I'd put the phone down. 'You know....'

Anyway, Twin Sister said she had to go. She had to get home.

Before she left, I wanted to say to her I was sorry that she was the only one who'd had to admit to having an affair with J., that it was hardly fair, seeing as she had called the meeting.

Then the phone rang. 'It's Ivor,' Twin Sister said, holding out the receiver.

Ivor said he would have to agree with Twin Sister. That I had a clear choice now: either break off all contact with her family, with J., with London Sister and J., and get on with a new life, or—

'I'm not the problem!' I half-shouted, half-cried, down the phone.

'You'll have to be very careful not to *become* the problem,' said Ivor.

'The *problem,*' I shouted, 'is my fucking sister is having a fucking affair with my fucking husband and my whole family is support-ing—'

'She certainly seems to have a lot of power within the family,' Ivor said.

'I have to get the truth out,' I shouted. 'I *have* to.'

Either that or I die, I thought, as the baby, kicking and wriggling, scrambled down.

When Twin Sister left I hunted high and low for the piece of paper I'd written the ad on. Then I gave up. It must have got lost in the chaos of 'stuff'—bottles, nappies, babygros. Then I forgot about it.

6

There was one thread left hanging. Pretending innocence, I rang London Sister : What did she mean when she'd said down in the Ladies that I didn't have 'an ounce of compassion'?

Taken aback, London Sister started chattering away. As if we were the best of best friends! 'Oh, you know, I just was—' , then as if to emphasise aren't we truly besties, she said: 'You'll never guess who was already here! Upstairs in bed, when I got back!'

My heart nose dived. *OhmyfuckingGod.* I dropped the phone.

In the morning I rang London Sister.

'Hi.'

'Hello'

I stiffened.

'Can I ask you something?'

'Of *course!*'

'Eh, do you love J? Are you *in love* with him?'

London Sister hesitated for a moment, then gushed, 'Yes, yes I am!'

The phone was snatched from her. J. came on the line: 'What the fuck do you think you're doing? Get off this fucking line, *now.*'

I placed the big black receiver on the table, J.'s voice, an angry trapped wasp's, still buzzing furiously.

I rang Eldest Brother. I told him J. was at London Sister's house when she got back. 'Ah for god's sake.' I tried Second Eldest Sister, Second Youngest Sister, Youngest Sister. None of them picked up. I rang Mum.

'Well you were horrible to everyone at that meeting yesterday,' Mum said. But she didn't have time to talk. She was on her way to meet her daughters for coffee in town.

'J. is at—'

But Mum had already put the phone down.

I rang Twin Sister. 'Jesus Fucking *Christ*' her husband shouted.

Upstairs I shoved nappies, baby clothes, jeans into a backpack. 'We're off on an adventure!' I said to my little daughter. 'We're off to stay with Twin Sister and the cousins! How about that?'

'We're going on our holidays!' my little daughter said, leaning in over the baby. The baby gurgled, fat hands clutching at her swinging hair.

It wasn't easy. Five small children. A Mum and a Dad working flat out in the workshop next door to the house, the muffled roar of the machines going all day. A broken, penniless Mum dragging her broken self and her two children through the days to social workers, solicitors, a tarot reader, a therapist.

One afternoon, in the bedlam of small children, the television blaring, a hoover, a scream as someone's bare foot stood on a piece of Lego, the phone rang.

'It's Ivor. For you.' Twin Sister held out the phone. I took it cautiously and sat into the sofa with the baby.

'Ivor here,' said the familiar voice, 'there've been some developments.'

J. had come back. Had driven up home. Had found his nest empty. Bird and chicks flown. Had driven into town. Booked himself into the Shelbourne Hotel and had a nervous breakdown.

'God!' Twin Sister exploded when I relayed the phone call. 'Who *cares*? I hope he has twenty more breakdowns!'

I followed her into the kitchen. 'What's the—?'

'Watch out!' Twin Sister grabbed my arm. I stepped back, almost falling over the bulging laundry basket.

'What's the matter?' I asked, as Twin Sister, butt in the air, threw things around under the sink. She looked back over her shoulder: 'What the hell do you care if he has had a breakdown or not?'

I backed against the far counter. 'I don't know. It's just, you know, at least he cares that much—' my voice trailed off.

Twin Sister slammed the cupboard doors shut. 'He probably just stopped taking his medication.'

I was about to say he's not on any medication, but Twin Sister was already gone, shouting at one of the children to Put That Down. *Now.*

As the evening reached its domestic crescendo, tired kids, tired Mums, tired Dad, supper preparations underway, television still blaring, Twin Sister's husband looked over as he swiped chopped tomatoes, mushrooms, green beans, mangetouts, garlic, into a wide pan.

'J. isn't having such a bad time of it, is he?' he said as he reached back to put the chopping board down. 'Breakdowns in posh hotels, two doctors hanging on his every word, eating out on a nightly basis, while other people look after his wife and kids?' He peered forward into the hissing pan, turned to look at me over his glasses.

'I suppose,' I said, 'yeah.' Wishing the ground would open and swallow me up. Wishing the ground would open and swallow him up.

Phone calls from J. started the following day.

I love you I love you do you know how much I love you? I miss you—it's agony being here without you and the kids—it was all a terrible mistake—I can explain everything—I just went to her house because it was late at night—I was right off a bloody eight-hour flight absolutely knackered—I had nowhere else to go—I had no idea it would—such uproar—I love you I want you—how are the kids?—tell them I love them tell them—I want to see them—

The phone pressed into my ear, I heard sobbing.

I've got to see you—and the kids—I don't know what's going to happen to me if I can't—I don't know what I will do to myself. More sobbing.

It was nighttime, the children in bed. Twin Sister, noisily tidying the sitting room, punching the sofa cushions, throwing items of discarded children's clothing towards the laundry basket, stopped in front of me: 'So it's all lovey dovey now, is it?'

Stung, I said: 'I'm just trying to play it by ear? You know? Take it step by step?'

Twin Sister grunted, throwing a plastic dinosaur into the wooden toy box under the stairs.

'It's like driving very fast in the dark,' I said, 'with no headlights.'

'Whatever,' Twin Sister said, not looking around.

She threw dolls, stickle bricks, a facecloth, bits of railway track, in on top of the dinosaur.

'I'm just trying to work out what to *do,*' I said. 'And,' I added, 'for my children and I to survive in the process.'

Twin Sister bent over, sweeping scrunched up tissues, broken biros, bits of Lego, into a battered, blue tin dustpan, and said: 'Your problem. Thanks be, not mine.'

It was New Year's Day morning. A pale blue, cold sky with high thin clouds. Pulling the coffee pot towards me at the breakfast table, I said: 'I've made a decision.'

Twin Sister and her husband looked up from behind their Sunday papers.

'I've decided to go home,' I said. I poured coffee.

Husband smashed his paper down into his lap. 'What?'

'I've decided to go home,' I said. Putting the pot down, handle angled towards them. 'Coffee?'

'Isn't that a bit—?' Husband began.

Twin Sister leaned forward, reached out a warm, work-rough hand, 'Listen, just because of what I said the other night—'

'Jesus!' I said, 'I'm not *that* sad!' I spooned honey, aware of husband and wife exchanging glances.

'It's New Year's Day,' I said, 'I'm going home to see if I can get my marriage sorted' I pointed to the horoscope page in one of the magazines and read: *'Only you can sort the mess Gemini! Go sort it!'*

'You can't make decisions based on the bloody stars in a Sunday paper!' Twin Sister said.

'Well,' Husband said, 'it is her decision to make....'

Twin Sister got up and began crashing plates into the sink.

7

'You've come back!' J. ran out across the grass, pushing his face in through the open car window. 'I thought you never would!' He clutched at me, kissed the side of my head, opened the car door, pulled me out. 'Hold me, feel me, I'm shaking all over. *Hold* me.' The children watched silently from the back of the car.

The baby in my arms, my little daughter in her Dad's arms, his free arm around my shoulders, J. led his family across the grass and into their home.

'I've got a fire, I've got wine, I've got dinner!' He squeezed us all in a lumpy embrace in the hall. 'I can't believe it! You're *home!*'

Sitting at the round table, a bottle of wine opened, our little daughter on his knee, J. leaned down: 'Isn't this nice? All of us together again. Me and Mum and you and the baby, a proper family!'

'And Vinegar.' Our little daughter held up her doll.

'Good Lord!' J. exclaimed, 'How could I possibly forget the famous Vinegar?'

Our little daughter smiled, looked down, smoothed Vinegar's crumpled blue cotton skirt. 'Silly Dad,' she said.

'Illy Da!' said the baby.

'Illy, illy, illy Da!' said J.

Down by the fire his teeth started chattering. 'Anxiety attack,' he castanetted through bared teeth, 'Need warmth. Hot water bottles. Duvet. More fire.' Swaddled in a duvet, the fire blazing, J.'s bare feet, inches from the flames, were a rooster's claws, stiff, orange and yellow. 'Promise me you'll never disappear like that again,' he said, bottom lip jutted out, tears running down his face. 'I couldn't take it. I *couldn't.*'

'Promise?'

The children played on the rug. Famous Vinegar's clothes laid out in a row, as the baby, one bare leg hooked under him, the other propelling him forward, rushed his favourite, yellow postman's van, around the kitchen floor. Grrrrr. Swsshhh. Be-eep.

The children asleep, I changed my clothes, put on some lipstick, came slowly back down to the kitchen.

J. was leaning against the Aga, long-legged, brandy glass in hand. Contrite, weeping, trembling Mr. Care Bear had transmogrified into Mr. Wolf. All grin, bulging eye, bright red tongue. He pulled me in against him. 'Mmm, mm...' he murmured. 'You feel like a dancer. All trim and taut.'

'So,' he said, holding me away, 'What's all this I hear about what you've been saying about London Sister and me? Eh?'

I gave a quick look into his gleaming face, his delighted eyes: 'How do you mean?'

'Oh-ho!' J. chuckled. 'Dropping information like chocolate drops behind you as you went!'

I scanned his face quickly. Looked quickly away. Away from his delight. His tickled pink, I-am-too-gorgeous-for-words, delight.

Chocolate drops, I thought as his hands pushed up my top, 'Oooh go on, give us a feel then.'

In the morning, I brought up the chocolate drops. What exactly had J. meant? J., in expensive blue and red striped towelling Liberty bathrobe, was cooking his family their breakfast.

'Don't let's discuss any contentious issues now,' he said, jiggling the frying pan into frantic activity. 'Let's keep contentious issues for when we're with the shrinks, hey?' He leaned down to adjust the flame below the pan. 'God knows, I'm paying the buggers enough. Okay?' He half-turned, holding up the egg slice in one hand, an empty plate in the other: 'Who's first for breakfast?'

I cut into the soft membrane covering the baby's egg. Warm yellow yoke flooded the plate. 'Goggy,' said the baby, digging in his spoon.

'Coffee?' J. asked, fussing with coffee pot and strainer. Standing over me, a fresh tea towel snapped over his shoulder.

'Okay? Everybody happy?'

'Vinegar is happy, Dad.'

J. laughed loudly. 'Three down, one to go.'

8

Our little daughter ran ahead of me: 'Dad! *Dad!* Mum has broken her face Dad!'

J. looked up.

'What the *fuck*?'

'Depilatory cream,' I muttered. 'I must be allergic.' A burning swelling rash covered the lower half of my face.

Bent over, slapping his thighs, J. pointed. 'Ha! Ha! Ha! Ha! What were you *thinking*?'

I was thinking, frantically, I *must* look good for the new shrink. A woman good looking enough not be deceived.

The Psychiatrist, appointed by Ivor who couldn't do it himself as I was 'technically' under his care, was sitting by an electric coal effect fire, watching intently as J. and I came through the door.

J. strode in, hand outstretched: How *was* the good doctor? How had the house party been? Nice suit by the way! *Excellent!* He sprawled across the armless settee, theatrically at home, at ease. I was waved to an ugly armchair opposite Mr. Shrink. I sat, imprisoned behind my burning, swollen face, and began, grinding out a tense, awkward account of how I thought 'all this' had started.

How J. and I and London Sister and her husband had known each other 'forever.' How we had always stayed at theirs—often for weeks at a time. But then J. started travelling on his own, and his visits to London became more frequent. Then London Sister's husband was drinking. And taking loads of pills. Convinced his failing marriage was all his fault. How my family all supported London Sister. Even when I told them what J. had told me, that he'd been 'frigging' her for years and years and she loved it—

J. bit his lip and turned away. *'For crying out loud!'*

'So you have been together a long time?' the shrink said, his eyes flickering over my rash-covered face.

'Twenty years!' J. said. The shrink looked briefly across at him.

'Everything changed after the children were born,' I said.

It was our third visit.

'I'll say,' J. said sourly, noisily shifting position on the settee 'After our daughter was born I had this sort of breakdown—'

The shrink's yellow eyes watched, unblinking.

'I discovered I was in shock,' I said. 'I wasn't *feeling*. To become a good mother, I had to get out of shock, I had to—'

'Give me the old you any day,' J. said, looking over conspiratorially at the shrink, 'An altogether easier entity to deal with!'

'Perhaps you had a *breakthrough*?' the shrink said, 'not a breakdown?'

'On her own up there in the bloody boondocks,' J. put in bitterly. 'Trying to give herself open-heart surgery.'

'I found out what was wrong with me!' I said.

'You were fine as you were,' said J. He threw himself back into the sofa.

'I was in shock!'

'So you say,' said J.

A fourth session. One, tufted eyebrow elevated, the Psychiatrist said, 'You are saying you knew about this, uh, *relationship*, between your husband and sister but you did nothing about it?'

'Nobody would believe me!' I said. 'My family all said I was mad.'

'Mad as a bloody brush!' J. said, nodding his head vigorously at the good doctor who held aloft a glass jug. 'Water, anyone?'

I took a glass. J. said it was a very long time since he drank water for pleasure, thankyouverymuch.

'Perhaps that's enough for one day,' said the shrink, looking at me out of the corner of his eyes.

'Everything was fine until the husband walked out,' J. said suddenly.

The shrink stared at him: 'I thought we said—'

J. got abruptly up. 'I'm getting extremely bored with all this.' He picked a newspaper off the table, dropped it again. 'I'm going out for a walk. When I come back I would like five minutes alone here.'

'*Alone,*' he repeated, standing over me.

The shrink and J. stood side by side as I got the children into their jackets.

'So,' J. asked, 'a prognosis so far?

'Hmmm,' the shrink said, 'Certainly a classic case of sibling rivalry.'

J. nodded sagely. Sure. Absolutely. Classic Sibling Rivalry.

I walked out to the car, my brain a machine smashing itself to pieces: *Sibling fucking rivalry?*

On the way home J. said he was 'making a diversion.' He was taking his family out for lunch. 'A *decent* lunch.'

A waiter, in linen apron, approached across a hushed carpet, to show us to a table, gleaming with glasses, silver cutlery, fresh flowers. A bentwood high chair was brought for the baby. A cushion for our daughter. The waiter poured chilled white wine into large thin glasses.

'Dad?' our little daughter said suddenly as J., very pleased with himself, was generously buttering a toasted slice with a curl of yellow butter, 'Why do you like London Sister?'

J.'s knife snapped the toast in half. He took up a stiff, snow-white napkin and flapped it open, gave me a look, turned to our daughter, and said, 'Who says I like her?', pushing his big laughing Dad face down to hers.

'Because you're always going away to see her,' she said.

J. straightened up. 'Despite what your mother *thinks,'* he said, looking across at me, 'I go away to *work.'*

'Mum says—'

'Oh look!' J. said pointing, 'Here come our yums!'

'In spite of what you *think* is going on,' J. said in the car, shoving the key into the ignition, 'I will see whoever the hell I want, whenever I want to. Right?' He revved the engine.

'So what is going on?' I said, sitting in the back with the children.

'*Nothing* is going on,' J. said, reversing out into the road.

In the driving mirror he tapped his forehead: 'It's all in there, love. Full-blown paranoia. My theory is,' he said, looking in the mirror, 'and many, *many* people agree with me, if London Sister didn't exist, you'd have to invent her.'

In the back of the car, our little daughter was counting approaching traffic by their colour as they rushed towards them. 'Black! Blue! Yellow! How many blue cars is that Mum?'

J., pressing down on the accelerator, said again into the driving mirror: 'You're crazy, Zibb. Screwed up as hell.'

Many, *many* people, I thought.

9

J. said he had made plans to travel again. Standing in the middle of the kitchen, shouting: 'How the hell can anyone know if I'm even alive, stuck out here in the middle of fucking nowhere?' He took a glass down from the wooden drainer over the sink.

I sat at the table, the baby on my knee; our little daughter kneeling on a chair beside me, looked up from her drawing. 'Why is Dad shouting, Mum?'

'Who do you think is going to keep this whole fucking circus on the road if I don't?' J. went on. 'You're not exactly at the peak of your earning powers.' He looked across contemptuously. 'And,' he said, putting a glass down on the table, 'thanks to your bloody hysterics I can no longer stay at your sister's.' He pulled a cork with a single, expert draw.

Upstairs he threw his suitcase on to the bed, ripping open both zips simultaneously. I sat in the window, holding the baby on my lap, trying to work out where all this had suddenly come from. Our little daughter did one of her humming songs: 'The Dad is cross. The Dad is shouting. The Dad is throwing his clothes on to the bed,' as she tucked her doll into a shoebox bed on the windowsill.

'Well?' said J. 'Do you want to check what I'm bringing or what?'

The next morning I asked: 'So are you planning to stay at London Sister's?'

'Maybe., J. said.

'So everything is cool again?'

'Meaning?'

'Meaning there's no reason why the children and I shouldn't come over too?' I said. Quickly. Lightly.

J., stacking up reports, shrugged his shoulders.

I dialled London.

'Hi. It's me!'

'He-llo...,' said London Sister.

Talking fast I said J. had to come over for a meeting. Just for a few days. I was thinking of coming too, bringing the children. All those fun things for them to do in London! Would it be okay if we all stayed?

Silence for a few seconds, then, a clipped: 'Yes. Fine'

'You sure?'

'I said yes,' said London Sister. The phone went dead.

Twenty minutes later I had tickets booked. 'You're *mad*!' J. said, shaking his head, smiling, walking out into the garden, the baby in his arms.

I phoned London Sister back.

Her son answered. Laughing, 'O Hi there! Can you hang on just one tick? I'll have to close the door!'

In the background, I heard crashing sounds, yells, more crashes.

'Is something wrong?'

'O it's just Mum,' London Sister's son said cheerfully. 'She's had a call or something. Some client she doesn't want to see. She's been crashing around the house like a madwoman ever since.'

'Oh,' I said.

'She threw the hoover down the stairs a minute ago!' London Sister's son said, laughing away.

'*Oh.*'

Outside, J. was pushing the baby in the yellow swing. Our little daughter dancing at his side. 'Me! Me! *Me*, Dad.'

'Family fun' I said to J.

'Indeed' he said, pushing the baby up and up into the blue sky.

Inside I heard the phone. 'Hullo!' I said cheerfully.

'Just what the *hell* do you think you're doing?'

'Sorry, what?'

'Just what the hell do you think you are *playing* at?' said Second Youngest Sister. *She* had been planning to go to London Sister's. For *months*. She had told me weeks ago. Didn't I remember? Of course not! This was *typical* of my behaviour, of my *stubbornness*, of my *selfishness*.

'I had no *idea!*' I said.

In spite of knowing *all* this, Second Youngest Sister went on, I *still* had decided to go and push myself in where I was not wanted. *And* totally destroy her plans.

She paused for a second. 'You like living on your nerves, don't you? It's not as if London Sister doesn't have enough to cope with at the moment. Her son is not a bit well. He's very disturbed by all these terrible accusations flying around.'

'I spoke to him this morning,' I said. 'He sounded fine.'

'O yes,' sneered Second Youngest Sister, 'Everything sounds *fine* to you. As long as you're getting what *you* want.'

I told J. when he came in. '*Christ,*' he whistled. Then putting the baby into his high chair, 'You can't blame me if all your sisters are psycho.'

I phoned Twin Sister when J. had gone down to the pub to get a bottle of wine.

'So bloody what?' Twin Sister said. 'Do what you want to do. It's a free country.'

'By the way,' Twin Sister said, 'why do you want to go over there? I would have thought that was the last place on earth—'

'If I stand in her house, I'll *know*. Anything would be better than this.'

'This what?'

'Oh come *on.*'

For once, Twin Sister shut up.

When the children were in bed, J., already settled into an armchair with a glass of brandy, remote in hand, the fire lit, was waiting to watch the video I'd picked up earlier in the village.

'And note you, Miss Suspicious Mind,' he said, 'the husband

comes back. Everything works out. Okay?'

'So you admit it?'

'I admit nothing. Can we just watch the bloody thing?' I knelt down, pressing the video into its black letterbox slot. 'I've been here non-stop for the past six fucking weeks haven't I?'

10

There was to be a family party! London Sister was coming with her husband and her son. Could I handle that? Second Eldest sister's voice on the phone was both solicitous and threatening.

J. walked into the kitchen, stretching and yawning. He had absolutely no problem about seeing London Sister. Or her husband. Why would he? He went over to the cupboard to get himself a glass.

I stopped cutting up the baby's lunch: 'Are you listening to every conversation I have on the phone?'

'Of course!' he laughed. 'Drinkey-poo?' he asked, holding up a glass and bottle.

Two days later, J. came into the kitchen again. It looked suddenly as if he was going to have to go away. Shame about the party, but there you are, he had no control over these things.

Two days later it turned out his trip was scheduled for the day *after* the party. He could still come. Was I mad? There was no fucking way he was driving a forty-eight bloody mile round trip to drink cheap red wine, talk to a bunch of people he had absolutely no bloody interest in, be up half the night and then have to get up and travel at five o'clock the next morning. No fucking way. Thankyouverymuch.

It was the day before the party. J's trip had been postponed again. He could still change his mind. I stood at the door of his study, our daughter at my side.

'Is there something specific you wanted me for?' asked J.

'Mum really wants you to go to the party,' our little daughter said, 'Don't you, Mum?'

'Mum is mad,' J. said.

I pressed my black satin pants. Slid into the fitted black velvet jacket my friend had lent. Cleaned my red patent stilettos with Vaseline. Snapped on a choker of pearls. Painted my nails. 'Bloody *hell*,' J. said. 'Hurry home to Daddy-o!'

At the front door, holding the baby, he called out, 'And don't you be late home young lady or you'll hear about it from me!' As if everything was normal. As if we were Adam and Eve, blissful in our leafy bower with our beautiful babies!

Coo-ee darling! *Coo-eeeee!* Maybe the party wouldn't be so bad after all.

London Sister's son opened the door. 'It's *her!*' he called back over his shoulder into the crowded house. I heard scurrying.

'Where's J. then?' London Sister's husband asked loudly, swaying up unsteadily from the sofa beer can in hand. 'Couldn't take the heat?' Hahaha.

Mum, sitting on a sofa just inside the door, looked up, 'Why didn't he come with you? I thought I'd told him to.'

Mum had rung J. and told him to come? I was handed a glass. London Sister, watching from the far corner, smiled. If she had been a dog, her tail would have been thumping the ground.

An embarrassed, sticky silence spread out like a stain around me. I fled to the bathroom. What had I been *thinking*?

Downstairs music started, its muted boom coming through the floorboards. If only I could sneak out without anyone seeing. The bathroom door handle rattled. Second Youngest Sister's voice said, 'Get a move on, whoever's in there.'

I didn't breathe.

'Is that you, Rosita?' the brass doorknob jiggled furiously. 'Oh you're such a *child*.'

Downstairs the double doors had been opened, the carpets rolled back, 'Sister Sledge' on the stereo. London Sister was holding tightly to Second Eldest Sister, jumping up and down, pink faced, holding my gaze as she yodelled the lyrics : 'We are family. I've got all my sisters with me!'

Twin Sister arrived. I sat beside her on the rolled up carpet.

'Bizarre, isn't it?'

Twin Sister watched intently. 'I don't know what it is exactly.'

'I think it's fucking weird.'

'So you said,' said Twin Sister.

I left after Mum had been put into a taxi. The car felt empty, cold. The full moon hammering down on a silvered sea. A fecund tang of seaweed as the song went round and round in my head—'We are family! I've got all my sisters with me!'—London Sister's set face, as she jumped updown, updown.

'How was the party?' J. asked in the morning, walking into the bedroom, the baby under one arm, holding out a tray with two mugs of tea. Our little daughter ran behind, 'Look what Vinegar is having for breakfast Mum!' she said, holding up a bottle filled with red tinted water. 'Dad says Vinegar is having blood for breakfast, didn't you, Dad?' Looking up, delighted, at her big, worldly, unshaven, bathrobe robed, tea-toting, baby-toting, Dad.

'Well?' J. said, letting the baby down onto the bed, handing tea, sitting himself companionably, 'how was the party?'

'Okay,' I said, my face bent to the tea, staring down into the swirling, opaque brownness, 'Alright.'

Our little daughter pulled at J. 'Come on, Dad, remember what you said, Dad?'

'Extraordinary!' said J., allowing himself to be pulled upright, 'For the first time ever, your *very* talkative Mum has nothing to say!'

'Dad! Let's *go*.'

'Talk to *you* later!' said J, bending down, kissing me noisily on the forehead.

There was a second party. This time for Youngest Sister and her friends. 'Here she comes!' shouted a voice as Youngest Sister appeared, smiling, holding up a glass to acknowledge the halloed greetings, pushing through the throng of bodies, John Denver on the stereo next door, 'You fill up my senses, Like a night in the forest, like a sleepy blue ocean....'

'Where's J?' I heard her saying as she got closer to where J. and I were standing, our backs to the counter in Second Eldest Sister's kitchen.

'Where is he?' I looked up to see J. grinning.

Second Youngest Sister turned to put her empty glass on the counter saying, 'I don't know what all the fuss is about. To me he's just like an uncle,' and walked away.

I felt a flash of fear: 'They all wanted to sleep with J?'

Second Eldest Sister stepped into Youngest Sister's path. 'Rosita is here,' I heard her say. She's here,' she repeated urgently, glancing back. Youngest Sister pushed her aside to make for J.

'Hi,' she said. 'How are ya?', standing there in a pale satiny, slippy, body clingy shift in front of J., freshly washed auburn hair, her beautiful young smiling face, tilted up to his: here I am, yum yum yum, ready to....

J. delighted, smiled, leaned down to deliver a kiss. Over his shoulder I saw Second Eldest Sister's shocked face. I looked away. I was a nothing. A blank space. My head ringing with white noise.

11

J. had gone to the village to get something for supper. An hour later the phone rang.

'I'm in the Royal!' he shouted. 'I'm having a lovely time! I'm with your friend Noelle.

The one and only!' he shouted. 'I've been introducing her to the pleasures of a very good Sancerre.'

I heard voices, laughter, then Noelle's piercing 'Who are you talking to darling? Come back here and entertain us immediately!'

'My audience awaits!' laughed J. 'See you later!'

Two hours passed, another, more slurred, phone call. 'O God, what are we going to *do*, Zibb? I can't live with you and I can't live without you.'

More laughter in the background, more loud voices.

Finally a scrunch scrunch, scrunch across the gravel, a shouted 'I'm ho-ome!' and J., lurching across the kitchen, put two bottles of wine and a packet of peanuts on the table. 'Didn't do sho well on the shupper front!'

Staggering back, he pulled a cork and poured and proffered a brimming glass.

'Come on!' he slurred, 'sdrink up!' emptying his own glass in one, banging it down on the table.

'Gett into the sprrit of schtings, Zibb!' he said, refilling his glass, splashing wine across the table. 'Arses up!' He leaned forward, breathing hard, then bumped glasses, splashing more wine, '*Schdrink?*'

He pulled me over to the Aga. Opened the lid. Flames licked upwards. Wrangling his ring off, J. held it over the fire. 'Will I drop it in, Zibb, will I?' I stared as he dropped the fat golden ring into the flames. A sharp fizzing noise as new yellow and green flames licked upwards. J. leaned across and grabbed my hand, pulling at my ring.

'Come on, Zibb! To hell with marriage and monogamy and adultery and faithfulness and all that crap! Chuck your ring in too! Come on, come with me! You're already up to your neck in it as it is!'

J.'s grinning face was lit up by leaping yellows and blues from the opened cooker: Mephisto standing at the entrance to his Paradise. His Inferno. Come!

'Take the ride, Zibb,' J. shouted. 'We'll ride the tiger together!'

Suddenly he stretched across and snatched the bread knife off the magnet on the wall behind me, unzipped his pants, took out his penis, held it, warm and flaccid, in the palm of his hand, laughing, 'Not the first time he's been out tonight!' He grasped my right hand, pushing the knife into it. 'Go on! Cut it off! You know you want to, Zibb!' His grinning face, inches from mine, breathed alcohol, garlic, tobacco. 'Go on!' he urged, jiggling his penis in his cupped hand.

I stared. I tried not to stare. I put the knife down on the counter behind me, pushing it back as far as I dared. Laughing, J. zipped himself back up. 'Too repressed eh, Zibb, eh?!'

Slamming down the Aga lid, he staggered backwards and crouched in the middle of the floor gorilla style, arms swinging, started banging gorilla fists on his chest.

'I want! I want! I want!'

Louder then: 'I WANT! I WANT! I WANT!'

Thump. Thump. Thump. Thump.

'EVERYONE KNOWS WHAT I FUCKING WANT!'

He began kicking the cupboard doors. The doors flying open with each booted kick. 'I'M GOING TO KICK THIS FUCKING

STABLE TO PIECES IF IDON'T GET WHAT I WANT!!! *NOW!!!!!!!!!!*'
I tried to not scream. To not look terrified. To keep him in the kitchen at all costs. To not let him upstairs where the children were. No matter what, to not let him upstairs where the children were.

Finally he sat, laughing, muttering to himself on the sofa, tearing his shirt open, buttons scattering across the floor, then slowly, slowly tilting sideways and down and passing out.

I crept upstairs. Pulled the chest of drawers across the door. Lay down. To sleep. To *sleep,* the children beside me.

12

Friends, with their 19-year-old daughter, just home from her first year at university in London, visited unexpectedly. They were sitting on a rug on the lawn, the wife waving, as I pulled into the yard. I left the baby asleep in the back of the car and went inside to make tea.

The husband said he was sorry to have missed J. How was the dear boy? What was he up to anyway? And, much more importantly, of course, how was I?

On an impulse, I decided to tell them of J.'s outburst three nights previously. The attempted, then aborted, trip to London Sister.

The wife listened, nodding sympathetically; the husband looked vague and embarrassed.

Their daughter, who in her year abroad, had metamorphosed from shy, grey feathered cygnet into proud young swan, was making a daisy chain with my daughter. She looked up, obsidian eyes sparking: 'But you *must* go over to London Sister's!'

Her mother looked at her, 'L.—'

'She *has* to go!' beautiful swan daughter insisted. 'There'll be blood and guts all over the place, but at least *she'll* be through.' She pointed at me.

I felt my heart beginning to beat fast. There *was* something I could do! Something I *should* do! I imagined exploding into London Sister's house, all guns blazing....

'She *can't*,' the wife said, placing a gentle hand on her daughter's arm. 'She can't bring violence in.' She gestured towards my little daughter. 'There are small children.'

From the car, the baby began to wail.

The next morning, I left the children with a friend and drove in alone to see the shrink. What if, I began, I travelled over, burst into London Sister's house, tore bald-headed into London Sister, shouting and screaming; there'd be blood and guts all over the place, but what did he—?

For a second the shrink's mask slipped, his sallow face paling to paper. He coughed, shifted in his chair, swallowed. 'And what, um, exactly would this *action* achieve?'

'The truth!' I said, hot all over.

'Aaah,' he said sitting back in his chair, 'the *truth*.' He rolled the word around in his mouth, eyeing me out of the corner of his yellow eyes.

I waited, inclined forward.

'You really think there is such a thing as the truth?' he said. 'Or is this perhaps your very black and white religious-bias education coming out? Neh?'

I flushed. 'Well, there is such a thing, isn't there? I mean? What is or isn't the *actual* situation?'

He nodded, 'Ach, yes, ze terrible trooth,' he said, his accent suddenly thick. '*Yah.*' He steepled his finger tips. 'I am more of the post-modern man myself.'

Whatever the fuck that means, I thought, driving home through blinding rain.

13

J. was back. He hurried into the kitchen after another long session on the phone. Who was he talking to? Ignoring the question, he rubbed his hands together. He'd just been offered this absolutely brilliant, once-in-a-lifetime-working-and-living opportunity. It was going to 'solve all our problems.'

He went over to the Aga. Busied himself with coffee pot, coffee, boiling water.

So. He'd been offered a two-year post in Kenya. Developing microfinance solutions for small businesses. It was a new, public-private partnership venture, with the possibility of 'making some real money.' It would, of course, involve 'relocation.' It would mean living abroad, for at least two years. Probably more.

What did I think?

'A new life,' said J. 'A big house. Swimming pool for the kids. Lots of servants. Plenty of sophisticated company when wanted or needed.' He pressed the plunger down into the cafetiere.

I was sitting at the table, the baby on my knee, hot and fractious after a night teething.

J. looked down disapprovingly. 'You'll have to get yourself into better shape, you know. In Nairobi you'll have a big house to run. Lunches and dinners to organise for colleagues. Visitors. I want a big, properly run establishment.' He looked sourly around the kitchen, out into the garden. 'The sooner we get out of this weed-infested patch the better.'

That evening, he was back on the attack. He didn't have time for splitting hairs. He had to get back on the road. Get out there, *network.* 'It's all very well for you!' he shouted, 'You've totally lost touch with reality! I'm a fucking gun for hire.' He stabbed himself in the chest with a stiff forefinger. 'Has it ever occurred to you,' he went on, 'the reason you can live like this,' he gestured, 'is because I go out and bust my fucking *arse* working. If I don't, you don't eat. It's that simple.'

He leaned forward. 'What's that you said?'

'I don't particularly want to live like this,' I repeated in a low voice.

'Well then,' he said, 'Accept fucking relocation.'

Two days passed. J. arrived back from a trip into the city, waving a piece of paper: 'You might like to frame this!'

I stared at an official looking certificate.

'HIV,' J. said, jabbing at the hand-written *'Negative'* at the bottom of the form. 'I'm in the clear!' He walked over to the fridge and pulled out a beer. 'At least you don't have to worry on that score!' he laughed, ripping the ring pull off the can.

'Why—?' I began, looking at the piece of paper.

J. snatched it back. 'It's for getting into Kenya, stupid. You have to be Aids-tested.'

But that wasn't what I had meant. J., not laughing, put the certificate into his briefcase with his other papers.

That night, we watched a film on tv.

A rich and sexy businessman, married, two kids, big posh pile in the country, sleek expensive vehicles parked on the deep crunch gravel out front. A gardener wheeling a barrow stacked with bedding plants. Everything hunky dory. Mucho pleasant lifestyle for Mr. and Mrs. Made It. On a business trip to Thailand, his hosts bring in 'ladies' after the business deal has been clinched. Everyone has a fan-fucking-tastic time. Six weeks later businessman is feeling 'off.' Tests begin. Businessman has contracted HIV. Very, very quickly it develops into full-blown Aids. Disbelief, Shock, Horror. Social Ostracisation. Hospitalisation. Wife falling apart. Family falling apart. Posh kids horribly teased in posh boarding schools. Rich and sexy businessman now a rattling skeleton in a huge old fever hospital hastily converted to an Aids hospice. Rich and Sexy businessman facing imminent and agonising death among the hollow-eyed drug users and the gays, those he once dismissed as the dregs of society.

J., leaning forward on the sofa, watched intently as the businessman's lovely life crumbled into shit.

'When are you going to make up your mind?' J. shouted as I hauled myself and the children back from a trip to the doctor. 'I am not, repeat NOT, going to spend another winter in this bloody place!'

The remainder of the day was spent on the phone. Click. Buzzzz. Click.

That evening, standing with his back to the Aga, he said, in a different, careful voice, 'Technically, you know, it will be desertion if you don't come with me.'

'Sorry?'

He lifted the lid of the Aga to throw in a balled-up piece of paper. 'Technically speaking,' he said, 'since you're not working at the moment, and I am the sole breadwinner, and I have to go abroad for work reasons, if you don't come with me, it will be desertion.' He smacked his hands together to remove imaginary dust. 'You are my wife, you know.'

I cut up the baby's fish fingers into small squares, a faint, but distinctive, fishy smell released with each small incision.

'Well?' said J.

'Well what?'

'Are you or are you not going to come with me?'

'I don't feel—' I began.

'You don't feel what?'

'I don't feel our marriage is fit enough to take us anywhere—'

'Bullshit!' J. shouted. 'You've been reading too many of those godawful self-help books.' He put on a mincing voice. How to Make Your Marriage Work, When Am I Going To Be Happy? Christ! Such *crap*. Where I come from, you just got on with it.'

My good feminist friend June Levine, partner to Ivor Browne, rang for a chat. Appalled when I told her about the Africa plan, she said: *'Please* tell me you are not going to go to Africa with that man where you will be cut off from all your friends and family, while he flies backwards and forwards to London and your sister?'

14

'You've got one month,' J. said. 'Then I'll be back to get you.' He leaned over the departure gate at the airport, for a quick, dry kiss.

Mum was hoovering her front hall when I arrived, the baby in my arms, my little daughter beside me. 'How are you?' I shouted over the noise of the hoover.

Mum had had a nasty flu.

'Oh,' Mum replied, not stopping hoovering, 'I'm fine.' She pulled the cord behind her as she turned a corner. 'If I can get through this, I can get through anything.'

I felt myself go slowly cold and sick all over.

Out in the car, rushing *roaring* away, my daughter's little white face in the driving mirror asked, 'What's wrong, Mum? Why are you crying, Mum?'

'It's, it's Granny,' I said.

164

'Is Granny really sick?'

I did a twisted smile. 'You could say that.'

I stood in my friend's kitchen. Described the scene in Mum's hall.

'Sweet Jesus.'

'She didn't even stop hoovering.'

'I know she's your mother,' my friend said, 'But she's a fucking bitch.'

'She's known all along,' I said, staring at my friend.

'Let's get fucking *annihilated,*' said my friend.

15

It was dark as we drove up home, the children asleep in their car seats, heads lolling together. I could hear the phone ringing inside the house, the answering machine's red light blinking in the window.

'Hello?' said a strangely altered sounding shrink. Drunk? Stoned? Both?

'Yes?' I said, suddenly sober.

'You were supposed to come see me this afternoon, yah?'

'I'm worried about money. We must owe you a small fortune by now.'

'You think only about money!' the shrink's voice shouted. 'I don't care about money! Money is not important to me!'

'All I meant was,' I said, stunned, 'J. left this morning. I really don't know what's happening—'

'I know *exactly* what is happening,' said the shrink. 'What is *going* to be happening.'

I clapped the receiver down.

In the morning our postman brought a card from lovely American Frank. 'Saw J. at your sister's last eve!' Frank wrote in his sloping hand. 'In FANTASTIC form! Never seen him better! Had the whole place in uproar! XXX Frank.'

The baby was colouring at the table with his sister's crayons, the crayon screeching as he did wider and wider loops around a little donkey's head.

I waited till evening then dialled J.'s hotel in Nairobi.

I was put straight through to his room.

Hi,' I said. 'It's me.'

'*Hello?*' J.'s voice sounded small, far away. Alarmed. 'What's happening?'

'You are not to come back here.'

J. started wailing. 'You can't do this to me, Zibb. You can't. You wouldn't treat a *dog* like this. Listen to me, Zibb, *listen*—'

I put the phone down on his accelerating protests.

I rang my friend.

'Good for you,' she said.

'I told the psychiatrist guy to fuck off as well.'

'Good,' she said, 'fucking collaborating piece of shit.'

PART SEVEN

'Why I remained so passive may seem peculiar to outsiders, but not to me. I was petrified and wanted us, my children and myself, to survive.'

Edna O'Brien, *Country Girl*

The next two days were spent cleaning the house. A physical, a psychological purging. A local woman came to help. The sun shone. The radio played country music, rock and roll—'The Sound of Loneliness,' 'Love's a Silver Bullet,' 'Stand By Your Man.' The two of them laughed as they crammed his expensive suits, his dry-cleaned shirts, his cashmere sweaters into black plastic bags. Burnt his blue aerogramme letters in a metal bin.

In the evening her friend had invited her and the children down for pizza. And wine.

She felt cheerful, she had energy, for the first time in months.

All would be well!

Driving back home in the dark from her friend's house, the children asleep in the back, the first thing she noticed was the lights. What? She was certain she hadn't left the lights on. Absolutely certain she hadn't left the house lit up like the Titanic. Lights ablaze in every window.

She drove slower now. A pitter-patter of unease growing inside.

What was going on?

As the mouth of the lane opened she saw the upstairs windows thrown wide. Music, Beethoven's Violin Concerto, a favourite, pouring out into the night. Discreetly parked under the big tree by the gate a bright red hire car.

Oh my God: her husband was back. And he was inside the house.

She turned the engine off. Turned off the headlights. Her heart now hammering out a tom-tom of frantic alarm: He's come back to kill me.

Wave of nausea. And fear.

Her little daughter woke up. 'What's happening, Mum?' Trying to make her voice casual, her heart beating so loud now it felt like the whole world must hear it, she released the handbrake, let the car roll backwards into the blackness, the gravel under the tyres going off like gunshots. 'We're going back to Libs darling.'

'But we've just left there, Mum!'

'I know! We'll go back just for a little.'

'But Mum—'

At the end of the lane she hauled the car around, moved slowly forward into the dark, PRAYING he wouldn't look out a window, he would be so high he wouldn't think to. PRAYING they would get away. Her friend wasn't exactly thrilled to see them back again. Not that she blamed her. Who in the real world welcomes a refugee mother and her two children on their doorstep after midnight? They made up a mattress on the living room floor. 'See you in the morning.'

She lay in the dark, adrenaline pulsing through, the beating of her heart so painful, no way would sleep come.

She tried to imagine what might have happened: he had rung London Sister from Nairobi. Relayed the delivered ultimatum. Understood this time it was meant. Understood lawyers and divorce were now inevitable. At that moment had he and London Sister decided getting rid of her was the only way out?

Get on a plane. Get back and get up to your home. Get rid of her.

Make it look like an accident. A fall down the stairs. Everyone knew she drank too much, smoked too much, cried too much for god's sake. The entire family was completely fed up with her. She was destroying the family! Snuffing out her pathetic little life would be a gift to everyone, the family could heal again, enjoy life again! As for the children, well they could be adopted, or given to Granny to bring up. They'd survive.

It was after six when she fell into a painful sleep. The phone was ringing, her friend standing over her. 'Your husband is on the phone.' His amused voice, as if all this were a play: 'I thought I'd find you there!'

She stood in her bare feet, the phone pressed tight. Didn't she want to come up to the house and get clean clothes for the children? Their toothbrushes? Their toys?

No.

He rang every hour. Could he speak to his wife, please? Why wouldn't his wife speak to him? Would she not even meet him for a coffee in the village? Nothing bad could happen to her in broad daylight, could it! What was she afraid of? Ha! Ha! Ha!

Even for him it was reckless. Openly admitting he'd come back with violence on his mind?

Two days later he announced a BIG surprise! He'd bought a house! Everything his darling wife had ever wanted! A Georgian fucking mansion overlooking the sea! She absolutely must meet him in the village so he could give her the brochure!

No.

'For fuck sake.'

He started going around her friends. Two, three bottles of wine. A bottle of brandy. The bright red hire car seen everywhere. Telling her friends how shattered he was. How desperately he missed his wife and his children. Crying big tears. That it was she who had run away AND TAKEN THE CHILDREN. Destroyed their marriage.

'You actually said that?'

He laughed. 'Well you have, haven't you?'

He drove down to her mother's house.

Her mother rang the next morning. 'Why won't you meet him? I do think you're being silly. What about the children? Don't they want to see their father?'

She couldn't, without sounding completely insane, tell anyone that she believed London Sister had sent him back to kill her. She certainly couldn't tell her mother.

That night when she was having a glass of wine in the kitchen with her friend she tried telling her. 'Are you sure?' *her friend said, eyeing her,* 'I mean really sure?'

Her friend's husband was even more sceptical. 'I know he's been a right
bastard to you and the kids, but a stone cold killer? I don't think so.'
She wished she'd said nothing.

There was no point in going to the police. What would she say?
Excuse me, officer but I have this feeling, this certainty actually, that
my husband has been sent back here by my sister to kill me so that she
can have him all to herself and—bonus points!—not get named in a
messy divorce which would be a very bad look on her shiny family law
lawyer's CV, not to mention him being obliged to pay alimony, actual
money, money they needed for their trips abroad! For their champagne!

A win, win, win you might say! The law was the law. She had left
the family home. She had taken his children away. She—

No, she couldn't bear to go through that rigmarole again.

By the end of the week, her husband had started to get ratty. 'Okay,
wander the fucking roads penniless for the rest of your life for all I care.'

She felt relieved. He was at last coming back down to earth. Back to
his bad-tempered, real self.

It was late in the evening when he rang again. Loud music, Bee-
thoven replaced by the Rolling Stones, 'I. Can't. Git. No. Satis-faction,'
high, laughing loudly, full of the joys: 'Don't you want to know what's
happening?'

'What's happening?' she asked, her voice wooden with tiredness.

'Your youngest sister is up here!'

'Sorry?'

'Well somebody has to entertain me!' He laughed loudly, shouting
over his shoulder, 'back in a minute!'

When she went back into her friend's kitchen her husband's eyes
widened, 'He's fucking another of your sisters?!'

Her friend thumped his arm, leaned across to fill her glass. 'He's a
complete asshole, so he is.' She pushed the glass towards her, 'So are

those bitches of sisters of yours.'

She felt a sudden flush of shame: her sisters, her family.

It was another week before he gave up and flew back to London.

When she and the children got back into the house it was filthy. A sniper's abandoned lair. His jacket, a bright red silk handkerchief lolling from the top pocket, on the back door.

Bags of rubbish in the kitchen. Bottles on every counter. The fridge empty apart from a triangle of cheese with a bloom of mould, sliced ham going neon-green, lettuce turned to a bad smelling brown liquid inside its plastic bag. Her LPs strewn across the sitting room floor sticky with splattered alcohol. In the spare bedroom a used condom on the floor underneath the bed.

The children, delighted, ran towards their trunk of toys. Soon they were sitting in a widening semi-circle of dolls, a yellow truck, books, teddies, puzzles, the tin spinning top that lit up and made music as it went round, going faster and faster across the tiled floor, 'Look, Mum! Look!'

PART SEVEN

'A family is a unit composed not only of children but of men, women, an occasional animal, and the common cold.'

Ogden Nash

1

Toddler baby on my knee, my little daughter on a rug on the floor with her favourite dolls, Pepo and Vinegar, I sat in the kitchen of a rented house in Cork, avalanches of nappies, bottles, runners, books, papers, socks, newspapers, dinner plates, cereal bowls, covering the counters, the kitchen table, the dresser, the chairs, the floor.

Upstairs, the beds were a tangle of sheets, wet nappies, clothes, some on the floor, more extruding from black plastic bags, more heaped on chairs. In the bathroom, cold, clouded water sat in a stained bathtub, strands of hair floating on top.

We ate jacket potatoes, the blackened roasting tin dumped straight onto the table, the butter, still in its crinkled foil, a knife stuck into it. Our clothes, hair, curtains, carpets, everything, sour with the smoke belching from a badly functioning anthracite cooker.

It was a Saturday. We were due to meet J. in a new hotel by the river. He wanted to see the children, he said. Bring my post. Bring *news*.

He sat alone at a table on a leaf-strewn, chilly patio, drink in hand, in the brutally sleek, barely completed hotel, perched on top of a steep escarpment, the river plunging and gurgling far below between steep rocky banks.

'Bottoms up!' he said, lifting his drink, all joie de vivre, as we approached.

'So what would everyone like to drink? Hey?'

The children sat watching. Unsure.

'Ah!' said J. grinning. 'Your post! I almost forgot!'—elaborately handing over two letters.

I took the letters, put them in my bag. Two letters in five weeks?

'I burnt the rest!' J. said, laughing.

But hang on, he was being daft! He really DID have exciting news! This very famous television naturalist had been out to look at home. He was TOTALLY interested in buying.

'Wouldn't that be *fantastic*? You know, lessen the pain of having to leave if you knew the person living there really loved it?'

I stared. He would really sell home?

J. was laughing again, pointing. 'You should see your face!'

'You're welcome to buy me out anytime you like, you know!' He laughed even more loudly.

'We haven't got—'

'You're doing it to yourself, Zibb!' He slapped his thigh, bent over with the hilarity of it all. Ha, Ha, Ha, Ha. '*You've* deserted me! *You've* taken the kids! You've abandoned our home!' He swirled his drink, making the ice clink merrily. 'Not that I give a shit' he said suddenly in a different voice, tipping the last of his drink into a back-tilted, opened mouth.

'You really are an out-and-out shit.'

'Yeah. well,' he said, putting his empty glass down onto the table.

At lunch, the children wolfed down plates of hot food. J. stared, 'They're *hungry.*'

Afterwards J. wanted to know what they would like to do. As if remembering he was Dad. They took the baby's new ball to the little wood at the side of the hotel, an imitation of Mum and Dad playing footie with their darlings. The toddling baby gurgling with delight as the gaily coloured ball rolled this way and that, as Dad put it on his head, pretended to run away. Our little daughter serious, holding tightly on to his hand.

Then it was time to go.

As I turned around from strapping the baby into his car seat, J.

let out a stifled, animal scream as he handed our little daughter over. Ashen-faced, unable to speak, his shirt crumpled where she had nested in.

As we drove away I could see him in the driving mirror, standing where we had left him, skeletal inside his expensive new clothes, one hand limply waving.

'*Why* does Dad have to go, Mum?' my little daughter asked that night, her face splattered with tears.

'O Darl.'

'But *why*, Mum?'

'It's because of Dad and London Sister, you know, they are having this, eh, relationship.'

'Doesn't she have her own Dad?'

'She got rid of him,' I said.

'She *killed* him?'

I smiled in the half dark, 'Not really. She just sent him away.'

2

A single-spaced, five pages long letter arrived from J.'s solicitor. The former 'family' solicitor.

'… in view of your client's insistence of meeting my client with the children in artificial settings, hotels etc., thereby inhibiting the possibility of a true father-child relationship developing, notice is hereby giving of an Application to the Courts for Joint Custody and full and free Access to the children, with three months holidays every Summer, ten days at Christmas and Easter....'

I ran over to Twin Sister and her Husband.

'Jesus fucking Christ, he's trying to get the *children.'*

My solicitor on the phone said they could fight off an access demand, easily. Of course, it would mean going to court. And, once the process was started....

Another letter four page letter arrived:

'...My client points out that he has no money unless he is working, and since he is unable to work at the moment because of your client's irrational behaviour, driving him to the point of complete nervous collapse, he is without funds. He therefore suggests that the liquidation of the family home would be the next logical step.'

'He's going to sell *home!*' I shouted down the phone at Twin Sister.

'Ring your solicitor!' She shouted. *'Now!'*

'Can't do it,' the solicitor said, 'Can't legally be done without your permission.'

A third letter arrived: 'It seems evident that it is your client's intention to achieve separation, on her own terms, having failed to substantiate earlier false accusations of adultery. In these circumstances, no useful purpose can be served by continuing efforts at reconciliation. My client is now seeking a divorce *a mensa et thoro*, grounded inter alia upon your client's desertion and upon mental cruelty, the latter with particular reference to the false accusations made in relation to my client's alleged adultery with your client's sister.'

'Maybe it's time we went for an opinion from one of the barristers?' my solicitor said.

A nappy-soaked, worn-out toddler on my lap, I sat opposite a large, beefy barrister chucking papers this way and that across a gargantuan, polished mahogany table: 'This bit of evidence is no good.' *Swish.* 'This is inadmissible.' *Swish.* 'This will not stand up in court.' *Swish.*

'No case,' the barrister said after twenty minutes, throwing herself back in her chair with massive creakings. She glared across, eyes bulged. 'All your husband has to say is that he's visiting your sister, they're just good friends, end of story.'

'But that's what he's been saying for years!'

'*Exactly,*' said the barrister.

'But—'

Solicitor and barrister conferred. The solicitor cleared her throat. The barrister had come to a (tentative) decision. If, and it was a very big if, *if* I could get doctors reports, reports from the police, reports from Ivor Browne, write down everything, all the ' incidents' with J., they might, they just might, be able to put together a case on grounds of mental cruelty.

'He's at my sister's right now,' I said, looking quickly away from my haggard reflection in the table below, 'He's left us without a—'

But the barrister had risen, was gathering her papers. 'Just concentrate on getting me those proofs,' she said, beating down her black skirt, grasping her stuffed briefcase under a meaty arm, laughing conspiratorially at the solicitor, 'and don't go telling me you haven't got a penny! We don't come cheap you know!'

Toting an exhausted toddler, in serious need of a clean nappy, I walked out through the labyrinth corridors of the Four Courts, through the marbled lobby, barristers rustling by in pairs, cloaks stiff, wigs tipped forward, all costume, business, go.

Back in Cork my little daughter, her face strained and stained with tears, sat in a baby chair. 'I've been here *all* day Mum.'

As if not moving would bring us back safely together.

3

The children in the back I drove into an eerily quiet housing estate on a hill overlooking Cork city, to meet a private detective.

It was Twin Sister's idea. 'It was fucking RIDICULOUS! J. was actually in London Sister's house, in her fucking bed, in her—' she stopped when she saw my face, 'it's time to get a private detective on the job. Past time!'

We were ushered down a prim pastel corridor and into an office. The back wall lined with steel baseball bats, a crossbow, a hatchet. Cameras, phones, walkie-talkies covered the desk.

Yeah, yeah, yeah, said the Private Dick, they could do all that stuff. Surveillance. Mini-cameras. Phone taps. Stakeouts. Bank account searches. Whatever. 'You name it, darling, we can do it.'

I explained that I, um, needed photographic and, umm, physical evidence of adultery, for, uh, legal reasons.

'No problem darling. We had a right pair of charmers only last week—living it up in the sunny south, champagne dinners, yachts, the lot—while the poor old missus and kids were left on welfare.'

He looked down at the photo I proffered. 'Oh yeah, I know the type.' He snapped the photo with the back of a none too clean fingernail.

I signed an authorisation form.

'Been together long, if you don't mind my asking?'

'Twenty years' I said.

'Ah.'

Then I wondered, did he mean how long J. and I had been together, or how long J. and London Sister had been together?

His 'team' would leave for London, on Friday morning. They'd be in touch as soon as they made contact. Right? 'You go home now love,' said the Private Dick, 'And don't you worry. We'll have this whole thing in the bag before Christmas Eve. A nice little Christmas present for yourself and the kiddies?'

Yeah, that'd be fantastic okay, photos of my, um, 'husband,' riding the bejaysus out of my Big Sis? Best Christmas present ever.

The down payment would be €170. 'Alright, my love?' I counted the notes out onto the crammed desk.

Three days. Three nights. Then the phone rang. It was the Private Dick. Any news? There was crackling on the line. Noise in the background. A woman's voice. Children. Music. 'I been there alright,' he said. 'Spent the night outside in my car. She was inside. Just her there, on her own. Making curtains or something, on a long table. No, no sign of himself. Nice looking girl, isn't she?'

Was, eh, was that it?

'The thing is....'

The thing was, it was Christmas, between one thing and another he had gotten back together with his Missus. Sounds of children's voices, a woman's voice, music, now made sense. He needed the rest of the money. I was a nice lady. I could understand that, couldn't I?

I was still standing, thinking, that's all our money gone, and, what am I going to do now? When Twin Sister rang. 'London Sister is over here! Gertie is giving a family drinks party for her on Christmas Day! We've been invited. Everyone has been invited! The aunts. The Wolfe-Flannagans, the cousins....'

I got a strange feeling in my head.

'Hello?'

'Are you there, Zibb?'

'Don't worry,' Twin Sister's Husband shouted into the phone, 'There's no way we're going to that bloody party.'

'Maybe I *will* go,' said Twin Sister. 'Tell London Sister what I think of her.'

4

Christmas morning. A sodden sky collapsed onto dripping hawthorn hedges. The children, in the big bed, reflected in the spotted mirror above the tissue-choked grate. News breaking on the radio: an unprecedented disaster, far away, hundreds buried alive in an overnight avalanche—children, grandparents, parents, teenagers, pets, engulfed inside their own homes.

A strange, stiff, purplish face, as if pickled in formaldehyde, looked out from the age-spotted mirror.

'God,' mouthed the face, a hand slowly coming up to the mouth, 'Is that *me*?'

5

J. was green when he stood in the witness stand in the courtroom in Wicklow. 'I *understand*,' the Judge said, looking down at him over the top of his spectacles, 'that you are taking advice from your sister-in-law, a solicitor, with whom you are living?' J.'s reply was inaudible.

Afterwards the barrister was triumphant: 'You got everything you wanted!'

Earlier in the lobby, she had been impatient: 'You do realise it's your family, your mother and your brother, that are feeding all this negative information about you to the other side?' I stood alone as she hurried away, files under her arm, gown billowing, high heels ricocheting off the tiled floors. *Your mother and your brother—*

6

It was Halloween! Our favourite holiday! We'd tied an orange balloon and a black balloon to the front gate. J. was due. His first visit in months.

'One, Two, three, Four' my little daughter counted out coloured sweets in front of the toddler. 'See? *See*?'

'One, two, twenty-one, fifteen, *three*!' called out the toddler, surprising even himself.

'*No!*' my little daughter shouted, 'Stop being *stupid!*' picking up the sweets to count them out again, 'One. Two—'

The phone rang.

J. He'd been in a 'bit of a' car crash. No, not with London Sister. No, he wasn't in London actually. He was 'away.' Working. He was with the um, he had been with the, um, friend of a friend, the um, wife of an, um, friend. And they had been in this, um, accident, and—

'Are you having a scene with her?'

'Yes.'

'Does London Sister know?' I asked.

'She does now,' J. said bitterly.

I drove into town to see Mum. Mum said she had rung London Sister and told her, 'That's it, you'll have to get that man to leave.'

Pandemonium reigned.

My God! Poor London Sister! Poor, poor thing! She was in the most terrible state! They were frantic with worry about her! They didn't know what she might do! That utter fucking *bastard!*

London Sister was having a breakdown. Loss of TONS of weight! Lots and lots of screaming! Massive tearings of hair! Nightly, and daily, cursings of God! Face down tantrums on carpets. The Bastard, the utter fucking *BASTARD!*

Poor, poor *darling* London Sister! What an *asshole* J. was.

Second Youngest Sister, in a suede mini skirt, sat on a high stool in Mum's kitchen, chain-smoking. Yes, she was *very* concerned. London Sister might actually, you know— She stared meaningfully, and accusingly, at me.

Second Eldest Sister was just back from London. They were taking it in relays to be at London Sister's side. She was not to be left alone 'for a second.' London Sister's husband, poor cuckolded husband, visited every day, bringing fresh flowers. Second Youngest Sister was due to fly over in the morning.

Second Eldest Sister, her face a fist, said, 'I wish we had never heard of that bastard's existence.'

My little daughter, looking up, asked, 'Who's she talking about Mum?'

Second Youngest Sister, crossing her legs, tights squeaking on tights, said, 'I always *knew* that man was trouble.'

'What man are they talking about, Mum?' my little daughter asked.

'Your *bloody father*.' Second Eldest Sister said, leaning down to spit the words into my girl's little up-turned face.

'Are they scared she's is going to kill herself. or what?' asked Twin Sister on the phone.

Days passed. I waited for someone to say something. Twin Sister rang.

'Is nobody going to say anything?'

'About what?' Twin Sister said.

7

It was Mother's Day. Mum had asked the children and I to visit. Sitting in her armchair, a large, fragrant and very beautiful bouquet of flowers and an expensive white wine from London Sister on her table, Mum gestured for me to sit down.

Second Eldest Sister, standing at the mantelpiece, watched the children and me out of the corner of her eye. Second Youngest sister sat in the sofa holding up a glass. 'Cheers!'

Mum got up to get another glass from the dining room.

Second Eldest Sister and Second Youngest Sister began talking. As if we weren't there. As if we didn't exist. I felt beads of perspiration burning in my armpits. The toddler began wailing: 'TV. Want TV!' I pulled him onto my knee. 'Not now. Not today.'

'You know you could let him Mum, if—' my little daughter began.

Second Eldest Sister and Second Youngest Sister stopped talking to watch.

'*No,*' I said.

Toddler wailed louder. Began pulling at my sweater. 'I'm going to the bathroom,' I said, grabbing him and getting up. My little daughter ran behind.

'What's the matter with *her*?' I heard Second Youngest Sister say.

'Oh there's always *something* with that one, 'Second Eldest Sister said. I heard Second Youngest Sister snort a laugh.

In the little bathroom, both taps running full tilt, the toddler, holding onto the bath, howled and beat his travel cup on the white enamel. My little daughter, her back against the locked door, hands over her ears, shouted 'Shut up, SHUT UP.'

My arms like electrified steel, I picked him. 'We are going home. *Now*. Right now.'

In the sitting room, I picked up my bag. 'I'm going to go,' I said to Mum.

'What?' Mum said, 'You haven't even had a glass of wine.'

'I don't want a glass of wine, thank you. I'm going to go.'

I could see my sisters exchanging glances.

'But why?' Mum said.

'You're not still going on about that husband of yours are you?' Second Youngest Sister said. She finished off her wine, '*Jesus!*' She looked over at Second Eldest Sister. She said, 'It's in the *past. OVER. Oh Vee Eee Arr.*'

I turned at the door. 'Still going *on* about it? Nobody has even admitted anything happened,' I said.

The toddler, quiet now, pulled at my top, 'Mum.'

'*Mum!*' my little daughter urged, pulling at my jeans. 'Let's *go.*'

'I do think—' Mum began.

'*You!*' I shouted, turning to Mum, 'You never once stood by me and the children. Not *once!*'

Second Eldest Sister put her glass down and advanced across the floor. 'Listen, if you've nothing nice to say to Mum on Mother's Day, I suggest you go.'

'Oh don't worry,' I said, ' I'm *going.*'

In the car, my heart pumping as if it would explode, the toddler started wailing again. I yanked the car into a layby, grasped the sides of his car seat and began shaking it. 'Just stop it, STOP IT,' I screamed into his face, ignoring my little daughter's shocked, 'Mum, *Mum!*'

8

Twin Sister rang. She and her husband were at Mum's. They were going to come up for a quick visit. Okay? The children were asleep by the time they arrived. Twin Sister took up position in front of the Aga. So how was I? Any boyfriends? Any wild times?

I stared at her. 'I feel about as sexy as a frozen fish finger.'

Twin Sister's husband laughed.

'For God's sake!' said Twin Sister. 'You can't go on obsessing about what happened for ever and ever. Anyway,' she went on, 'If London Sister hadn't gone off with J. somebody else would have.'

I opened my mouth.

'OF COURSE THEY BLOODY WOULD!' Twin Sister shouted.

I swallowed. 'What exactly do you mean?' I said, trying to put the pieces of my head back together.

'It *means*,' said Twin Sister, leaning forward, 'it was an *affair*. Now It's over. *Over.*'

'Hang on,' I said, 'London Sister hasn't even admitted anything happened.'

Twin Sister came over to the table, refilled her glass from the bottle she and her husband had brought, stepped back, said in a mollifying voice: 'Why don't you contact your old friends?' She took a mouthful of wine. 'Get your life going again!' She paused to light a cigarillo. Thin blue smoke curled up. 'You know,' she said, 'all modern psychiatry says that the primary function of the family, once the young have been raised, is to separate.'

She tapped ash into a saucer. 'A healthy family is a family that has learned to separate,' she said, taking another draw on her cigarillo, pleased with herself. 'So for heavens sake—'

The phone rang.

It was Mum. Were Twin Sister and her husband still with me? London Sister was waiting for them. She wanted to say goodbye.

Shaking, I put the phone down: 'That was Mum. London Sister is waiting for you. To say goodbye.'

Twin Sister ground out her cigarillo. Her husband's pale face flushed.

'Well—' began Twin Sister.

'*Out*,' I said, pointing at the hall door. 'Get out. *Now.*'

At the door, pushing her husband ahead of her, Twin Sister turned. 'I couldn't *bear* to be such an outsider,' she said, 'It's, it's *horrible.*'

9

I had a dream. A huge and brutal cement auditorium. Hundreds of people in banked seats shouting and cheering.

In the first part of the dream I am part of the audience. Then I am on stage. Then I am just a flattened, blackened mark on the stage boards. Like in Hiroshima. Nothing left of a human being but a stain on concrete. I feel scorched with shame: what I have been reduced to.

Twin Sister is standing over me, triumphant, laughing up into the audience. 'This is for the pleasure of the "higher ups",' she calls out.

The 'higher ups,' London Sister, Second Eldest Sister, Second Youngest Sister, appear side by side in the best seats, applauding Twin Sister. Clapping madly! Cheering!

I woke up. The horror of the dream sticking to me like cold vomit.

10

'We're going to visit Granny,' I said, 'Of *course* you want to go.'

'I want to stay home,' said my little daughter.

'We're going to get totally left behind!' I shouted, 'everyone is going to forget about us!'

Out at the car, frantic now, I forced my little daughter into her seat, furiously buckling. 'For heaven's sake! Stop being so *impossible.*'

The toddler threw his cup of orange juice onto the car floor.

'For fuck sake, guys!' I yelled, 'Here I am breaking my ass to get you a nice outing with Granny and—'

'We don't want to go, do we?' my little daughter said to her brother, bending forward in her seat.

'We have to integrate back into society,' I said into the driving mirror through clenched jaws. 'We fucking *have* to.'

190

Mum was waiting. She made tea, then sat opposite, making small talk, working on a baby jacket for one of the cousins' new babies. Did I know about it? No, I didn't. Mum's hooked needle bit in and out of the soft white yarn. Well, she'd had it three weeks ago. Now Mum was making it a jacket.

I talked. Paused. Talked more while Mum did buttonholes. The children, on the carpet, went through old, torn, already crayoned colouring books. I talked in a high, tense voice of catastrophes, fights, deaths, women and children in terrible circumstances; women being raped, a young woman being burned with acid by her mother in law. Mum worked her needle. Yes, she would have another cup. Just half a cup, thank you.

While Mum was out of the room I examined the mantelpiece crowded with silver framed photographs of Second Youngest Sister's children, smiling into the camera; of Second Eldest Sister and Second Youngest Sister, either side of Mum at the annual flower show. A fucking *flower* show. Mum on her holidays with all the sisters, including London Sister, including Twin Sister, on a pretty white bench in the porch of an old fashioned hotel, roses bending over the trellised wooden frame, as they posed, wine glasses raised. So jolly dee! So enjoying their lovely fucking holiday!

Back at home, I waited by the kettle, holding a hot bottle. The phone rang. I turned, scalding water pouring over the back of my hand.

My little daughter held out the phone. 'It's Libby, Mum!'

I stared down at rapidly reddening skin. I hadn't felt a thing. Not a *thing*.

'Mum is crying,' my little daughter said into the phone.

Upstairs when I'd finished reading *The Twelve Dancing Princesses*, I bent to kiss her goodnight. Her little face, white and solemn in

191

the darkness: 'Why does Granny hate us, Mum?'

'Oh *darling*.'

Downstairs I stood in front of the bathroom mirror. Maybe it would be better if I was dead? Better for the children? Of course it fucking would, the terrible face in the mirror jeered back.

11

I sat opposite the doctor, my little son on my knee, my daughter standing at the desk's edge.

'I feel awful,' I said. 'I'm in such pain all the time. I wake up feeling absolutely shite and I go—'

The doctor, stethoscope around her neck, white coat open over a softly expensive, lavender wool dress, looked across.

'If I could just get something—you know?'

'Mum shouts at us,' said my daughter.

The doctor laughed.

'All the time,' said my daughter.

The doctor, moving the plastic model of an opened heart, veins, arteries, heart chamber, carefully shown, out of reach, said to my little daughter, 'No need of RTE news with you around, is there?' She laughed.

'Some strong painkillers or something?' I asked, hating the sound of my voice.

'We don't really give out painkillers on an ad hoc basis anymore, you know' The doctor said, writing on her pad.

Ripping it smartly off she handed it across.

'Maybe you should try a holiday?' she said. 'You know, get away from it all?' She nodded meaningfully in the children's direction.

'I don't even have enough money to—' I began.

'Take care now!' said the doctor, as I fumbled at the door.

Out in the bare, tarmacadamed car park, sweet wrappers, plastic bottles, discarded condoms strewn among the nettles flattened against the wire fence, I sat in the car, banging my forehead on the steering wheel. 'Fuck, fuck, fuck, fuck, *fuck.*'

My little daughter, her small alarmed face in the driving mirror, asked, 'What's the matter, Mum?'

'What's the *matter?*' I snarled. 'Everything is completely and totally and utterly *shite.*' Snarling the terrible words into her. 'Everything in this whole fucking world is a fucking nightmare.'

12

It was early afternoon when the woman from the Department of Health called. The government was doing a survey on the Vitamin and Mineral Intake of Single Mothers with Young Children. I had been randomly selected. Would I be so good as to answer some questions?

I grasped the survey out of her hands and tried to rip the glossy sheets. Scattering the pages onto the grass.

'We don't need fucking surveys.'

'I'm just doing my job,' the woman said, backing away, fumbling to retrieve the scattered pages. 'I mean if—'

'Oh yeah, sure,' I said.

'I'm just doing my job,' she said again, trying to shove her clipboard into her briefcase. Said she would go now. It obviously wasn't a good time. She could finish the survey some other time. Alright? Okay?

'As if the government gave a *shite* about single parents, about their children,' I shouted as she hurried away across the grass.

'Vitamins!' I shouted, 'Are you fucking joking? We have €89 a week. A fucking *week!*'

13

It was midday when I rang the number my friend had given me. Standing out in the yard, one hand rammed into a thicket of unbrushed hair, I said, over loudly, 'I think I need to see someone.' The fresh east wind sent a plastic bottle rolling emptily, noisily, across the yard. 'Quite soon if that were possible,' I shouted, stiff jawed, into the phone.

Four days later I sat opposite a therapist.

'I yell at them, I smash their toys—'

Not breaking eye contact, the therapist reefed fresh tissues from the box positioned between us.

'How? How *could* I?' I wadded the tissues into a frayed sodden lump. Searched the therapist's steadfast brown eyes. 'My own *children*. 'I thought I'd been so hard done by, *Poor Little Me,* you know? Now I've turned into this, this *monster.*

'I sit in my kitchen at night, wishing I was dead; thinking my children would be better off if I was dead.'

The therapist put out a warm restraining hand. 'Don't ever say that,' she said gently, 'You're their mother.'

'That's. What's. So. *Unbearable.* The other day I saw myself through my daughter's eyes. I was standing over her, my arm raised, and I suddenly saw such contempt in her eyes. I saw me, this insane, towering inferno, of an insane mother. I ran outside. I thought, my god, what have I turned into? My own daughter has to protect herself, and her little brother against *me,* their mother.'

The therapist nodded, stood behind me, pressing warm hands down on my shoulders. 'Stay with it Rosita. Stay with the pain.'

I lowered myself into the vat of poison, of corroding guilt. I heard the children's cries. 'Stop it Mum!' 'Mum!' 'Come on Mum.' Sitting in the bathroom, body clenched, nails driving into the palm of my hand. 'I *won't* come on. I don't *want* to come on. I hate everything and everyone. I *hate* God. Fuck you God. You fucking, *fucking* bastard.'

Upstairs later, all the lights off, kneeling beside the big bed, whispering to my little daughter, to my little son: 'I'm so sorry, I'm so, so sorry.'

'It's okay, Mum.'

My head bowed over the small pale faces floating in the darkness, No, not okay. No, no, no, NOT OKAY.

It was my fourth session.

'What you are going through now is because of what you *have* been through, you understand that?'

'Um?'

'You were threatened to the core of your being by your husband, by your sister, by your family.'

'Now that the immediate danger is over, you've gone into post-traumatic stress.'

'Like a soldier?'

'Exactly,' said the therapist, 'Like anyone who's been at the mercy of terrifying events for a long time, over which they have no control.'

Lying on my back, I felt tears leaking out, running down into my hair.

At the fifth session, the therapist stood to the side: 'Who is judging you now, Rosita?' She leaned forward, '*Who?*'

I shook my head, 'I…I don't understand.'

'Who, now, in this room, is judging you?'

'I…I don't know.'

'*You* are' said the therapist.

My mouth opened. 'How many times can you tell your children

you're sorry? And then do the same thing again?'

'It doesn't matter how many times,' the therapist said. 'It's when they think that it's their fault that the damage sets in.'

As I drove home, I rehearsed what I was going to say. How I was going to say it. Where. I'd do it in the morning, the sun coming into the bedroom, all three of us sitting up in the big bed, my arms around them: Mummy has something very, very important to say....

No. Forget the bloody violins. Just do it. *Mean* it. The saying of it will be the start of change.

Fresh images swarmed: smashing the play cupboard door off its hinges. Kicking my little boy's lego warship so pieces flew across the kitchen floor and under the counter. Tearing the ribbons off my daughter's party dress—*while it was still on her.*

A horn shrieked.

I wrenched the jeep sideways.

'Wake the fuck up!' screamed a truck driver, his furious, shocked face framed in the high window, his huge bulk hurtling past with just inches to spare.

I sat by the verge, heart hammering in the ticking silence.

It was hopeless. No, it was *perverse.* How can you ask your own children to forgive you for being terrible to them? For tearing their world to pieces, three, four times a day? I felt a savage, visceral urge to turn around and plant myself in the lorry's oncoming path, tear straight into it, foot to the floor.

My mobile rang.

'Mum?'

'Hi darl! I'm, ah, I'm—'

'Libby and I made a cake!'

'Goodness!'

'Are you nearly home, Mum?'

'I'm just going through the village' I said, 'Nearly home. Nearly, nearly, *nearly* home!'

I moved slowly forward and out, the roughly tarred road creaking like burnt cinders under the wheels.

Nearly, *nearly* home.

Dublin, March 2025.

Acknowledgments

Huge thanks to my agent Ger who took me out to lunch and said, Your job for the next year is to write your full memoir. *Girl* took more than a year but changed me in every possible, good, way. I learnt the truth of what had happened by telling myself the truth.

Huge thanks to Sheena Joughin who was endlessly, miraculously patient, always there with insightful guidance and the warmest encouragement.

Thanks to Annette McNamee who sang her love for the manuscript down the phone one Christmas evening.

Thanks always to Ursula Browne, an archangel disguised as a therapist.

Thank yous to Libby and Paddy Meegan who saved us in the long ago.

Thanks to Maurice Sweeney who said the four golden words that are music to a writer's ears: 'Yes, I'll publish that.' And thank you to writer Lucille Redmond who introduced us.

Above all thanks to my darlings, Chupi and Luke. I've faltered so many times. You've never given up. Ever. I love you

Rosita Sweetman
Dublin, March 2025